FOLK KNITS

FOLK KNITS

MELINDA COSS

Trafalgar Square Publishing

NORTH POMFRET, VERMONT

For Ray . . . who started me
knitting in the first place

First published in Great Britain in 1990 by
Anaya Publishers Limited, Strode House
45–50 Osnaburgh Street, London NW1 3ND

First published in the United States of America in 1991
by Trafalgar Square Publishing, North Pomfret, Vermont 05053

ISBN 0-943955-43-2

Library of Congress Catalog Card Number
91-65126

Designed by Martin Atcherley
Photography by Peter Waldman
Co-ordination and styling by Lynn Walford
Hair and make-up by Paula Mannj
Fashion drawings by Elena Symeou
Technique illustrations by Coral Mula
With thanks to: Neal Street, Ravissant, Sarsparilla, Anohki,
French Connection, Benetton, Liberty and Litvinoff & Fawcet

Typeset in Great Britain by Tradespools Ltd, Frome, Somerset
Colour reproduction by Columbia Offset, Singapore
Printed and bound in Hong Kong

CONTENTS

INTRODUCTION

FOLK KNITS is my eighth knitting book, and, looking back, it seems incredible that by learning two simple stitches – knit one, purl one – many, if not all, of my dreams have come true. There can be no greater privilege than being allowed to earn one's living doing what one enjoys most, and in my books I have endeavoured to produce designs that I hope you have found enjoyable both to make and to wear.

The designs in this book draw their inspiration from folk art and patterns from around the world. The beauty of folk art is its sheer spontaneity, and this springs from the fact that it is produced by people with no formal art skills and only the most primitive materials to work with. Like music, lettering and painting, design changes in character with time and place, and its very nature means that it derives from the decorative shapes created in the earliest cultures. Since the cave paintings of pre-history, people throughout the world have used colour and shape as the basis of communication, expressing their individuality through decoration in homes and on clothes and personal belongings.

Perhaps the most important aspect of folk art is that the designs have not been diluted or made 'sophisticated' by attempts at elaborate execution. The approach is straightforward and joyous, and, in many cases, it contains completely free interpretations of naturalistic themes. Throughout Europe and Asia images of plants, birds and animals are reproduced in a multitude of styles and colours, each reflecting the natural resources and traditions of the people who produced them. The bold, geometric patterns used throughout Africa and by the Indian tribes of North America suggest the early accomplishment of weaving skills, while the painstaking handwork of the Middle East and India is evident in the intricate carpet and costume designs originating from those areas.

For a contemporary designer the textiles, pottery and carpets produced by peasant communities provide an inexhaustible wealth of inspirational material. The primitive bark paintings of Australian Aborigines demand to be reproduced, while who can ignore the glorious beadwork of the North American Indians or the rich, bold stripes of a bedouin tent? In this book my problem has been the amount of material that the limited space has required me to leave out, so I have attempted to produce a diverse range of designs in the hope that there will be something to please all tastes and to suit all levels of skill.

My limitations, however, should not be yours. Why not re-draw some of my outlines on graph paper and add your own motifs and colours? Provided that you use yarn that knits up to the tension specified in the pattern for the shape you have selected, there is no reason you cannot create your own stunning and original designs. Perhaps there is some fabric that has caught your eye, or an illustration in a book, or a piece of porcelain. If you have mastered the technique of knitting with more than one colour at a time, there is nothing to stop you completing any of the patterns in this book or adapting any of the patterns to suit the image of your choice. Alternatively, you could use Swiss darning to add motifs to existing sweaters or sew tiny beads on to plain or finely cabled knitwear in the North American Indian style.

The origins of knitting must go back almost as far as those of folk art, and if a traditional skill is to survive in this high-tech world, it is essential that we pass it on from one generation to the next. Knitting is a comforting, creative and therapeutic pastime once you have mastered the basic skills. There can be few hobbies that can offer so many glorious textures and colours to work with and such a wealth of inspirational material to base designs upon. All that is required to produce an individual and practical garment are a pair of needles, a bag of yarns and the courage to interpret, in colours and shapes, whatever image catches your imagination.

Knitting has given me a great deal of pleasure and satisfaction, and I hope that this book will encourage you to explore your own capabilities and to produce some exciting and original designs.

MELINDA COSS

TECHNIQUES

READING THE CHARTS

The black and white charts accompanying the written instructions for each garment show how the colour motifs and designs should be worked. Use the charts in conjunction with the written instructions, which will explain when and how the charts are to be incorporated into the patterns. The written instructions will also indicate which colours should be used and explain any symbols.

If you are not used to following charts, remember that each square represents one stitch, both across (that is, horizontally) and up or down (that is, vertically or in a row). The flat page is a graphic representation of the right side of your work – that is, the smooth side of stocking stitch – and wherever possible, the charts begin with a right side row. Knits rows are worked from right to left on the charts, purl rows from left to right. Unless the patterns contain specific instructions to the contrary, you should always assume that the charts are worked in stocking stitch.

TENSION

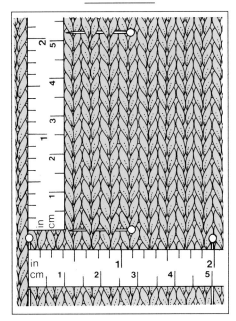

The single most important factor governing the success of any piece of knitting is achieving the correct tension or gauge. Tension means the number of stitches and rows in a given measurement using the needles and yarn quoted for a particular pattern. The instructions for each pattern include a tension measurement, and before you begin to knit the garment, you must work a sample piece, measuring at least 10cm square, using the appropriate needle size and yarn type and in the stitch specified. Cast on two or three more stitches than stated, because the edge stitches will not give an accurate measurement. When you have completed the sample piece or swatch, place it on a flat surface, taking care not to stretch or squash it, measure it with pins and a ruler and count the number of stitches completed. If you have too few stitches, you should work another swatch, using needles that are one size smaller. If you have too many stitches, use needles that are one size larger to work another swatch. Keep on changing needle sizes to work swatches until you achieve the correct tension. Remember that, if you use needles that are one size larger or smaller than those given in the pattern to knit the tension sample correctly, you must use proportionately larger or smaller needles than those given to complete all the parts of the pattern, including the ribs.

Because knitting patterns are worked out mathematically, it is essential that your tension is exactly the same as the tension specified in the patterns. Tiny differences over twenty stitches will be multiplied across the overall width, and the finished garment may be as much as a whole size too large or too small.

If your stitch tension is accurate, your row tension is likely to be very close to the specified measurement, and absolutely correct row tension is not, in any case, as crucial as stitch tension. However, if your row tension is slightly out, even though your stitch tension is correct, take care when working pieces like sleeves, which are calculated by row rather than by centimetres.

CASTING OFF

You will cast off not only at the end of your piece of work but also to shape blocks of stitches at shoulders and underarms. If you cast off a group of stitches at the end of a row, you will have to break off the yarn and rejoin it at the beginning of the next row.

On a knit row:

ONE.   Knit the first two stitches.

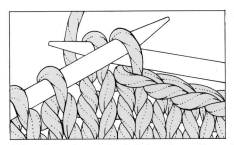

TWO.   Use the point of the left-hand needle to lift

the first stitch over the second, dropping the first stitch and leaving the second stitch on the right-hand needle.

THREE.   Knit one stitch.

FOUR.   Repeat steps 2 and 3 until the required number of stitches has been cast off.

When you are casting off to shape part of a garment, cast off the required number of stitches and knit to the end of the row. When you are finishing a piece of work, cast off until one stitch remains, cut the yarn to leave an end about 15cm long and pull it through the remaining stitch.

On a purl row:

ONE.   Purl the first two stitches.

TWO.   Keep the yarn forwards and repeat step 2 above.

THREE.   Purl one stitch.

FOUR.   Repeat steps 2 and 3 until the required number of stitches has been cast off.

If you are working a pattern, cast off by knitting or purling according to the pattern. If you tend to cast off too tightly, use a needle that is one or two sizes larger than you used for the rest of your work.

FAIR ISLE OR JACQUARD

The style of knitting that uses more than one colour in the same row to build up colour motifs is often called Fair Isle. Strictly speaking, the term Fair Isle should be used only to describe the type of knitting that involves small geometric patterns of the kind found on the knitwear produced on Fair Isle, and the word Jacquard is sometimes used instead. Nevertheless, the expression 'Fair Isle' is so widely used and is so generally understood, that it is used in the patterns in this book to describe the technique that should be used when two or more colours for small groups of stitches are used across one row. Some knitters are fortunate in being able to hold two colours of yarn simultaneously, carrying one in the left hand and one in the right, but most knitters will drop one colour before picking up and using the next colour, and the techniques of stranding and weaving described below assume that you will work in this way.

   One of the greatest problems with Fair Isle knitting is achieving the correct tension. You should always knit a tension swatch using the Fair Isle technique for any garment that involves large areas of Fair Isle patterns, and the elasticity of the Fair Isle areas should be the same as that of the other parts of the work so that the motifs do not become distorted.

Stranding

When you are working small pattern repeats of four or five stitches you should use the stranding method.

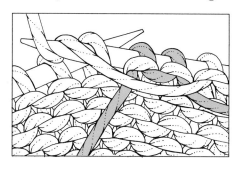

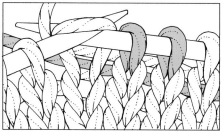

This system simply means that the yarn not in use is carried loosely along the back of the work until it is needed, when it is picked up and the first yarn dropped. You must always ensure that the carried yarn is not pulled tightly when it is knitted so that it does not make the work pucker. On the other hand, of course, you should try to avoid leaving strands that are so loose that they get caught when the garment is taken on and off. If necessary, stitch loose strands in place on the wrong side once the piece is complete.

Weaving

If the pattern you are working has large areas of a single colour before the next colour is required, you should use the weaving method, which involves looping the carried yarn under or over the yarn in use on every stitch. Carry the second yarn on the

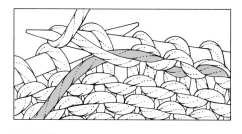

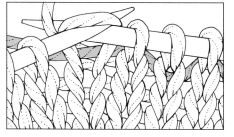

wrong side of the work over the yarn you are using for one stitch and under it for the next one. As with stranding, take care that you do not pull the carried yarn too tightly.

Many people find it easier to achieve an even tension with weaving as there is no need to assess the length of the strand. However, weaving does result in a thicker piece of knitting, which may not be desirable if you are using a heavy yarn, and it does increase the chances of the carried yarn showing through on the right side of your work.

Stranding and weaving

Unless you are knitting a small geometric pattern, you will probably find that it is easier to use both stranding and weaving as many garments have patterns that combine small and large areas of colour. Success will depend on ensuring that the tension throughout is uniform, whichever technique you use.

INTARSIA

The technique that is used for several large areas of a single colour is called intarsia. It is sometimes also known as mock patchwork or picture knitting. A separate ball of yarn is needed for each colour area, and if the same colour appears more than once in the same row, you may need to divide a ball or skein of wool into several small balls. One way of doing this is to wind the yarn around bobbins or pieces of card, and it is, in any case, sometimes helpful to use smaller balls of colour as several heavy balls may pull your work out of shape.

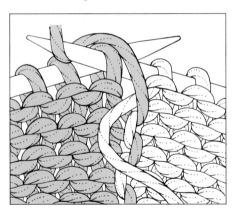

When you change colours, you must make sure that you twist the two yarns around each other to prevent holes forming. If you do not twist the two colours, there is no thread of yarn to connect the last stitch worked in one colour with the first stitch worked in the next colour. Remember to twist the colours together firmly so that holes do not appear when the work is finished.

There are two main problems with this technique. First, the small balls or bobbins of yarn tend to get tangled, especially when you are using several colours, and sorting them out at the end of every row can slow you down. Some people use small jars or boxes to help keep the yarns separate. The second problem is that every time you start and complete a colour area you will have two extra ends to tie in and finish off securely.

SEAMS

Making up your work neatly and using the appropriate seam will give your knitting the finishing touch. The written instructions for every pattern include details of the type of seams to be used and the order in which the various parts of the garment are to be joined together. Always follow these instructions carefully, and remember to change the colour of the yarn you are using for the seams to match the colours of the different parts of the garment.

There are four main ways of joining seams: by back stitch, by slip stitch, by flat seams and by knitting seams together. When you cast on and off, always make sure that you leave a sufficiently long length of yarn to fasten a seam off. This will avoid the problems arising from having to tie in and fasten off additional ends of yarn, which may work loose at the bottom of ribs or under arms.

Back stitch

Back stitched seams are strong and elastic, and they can be worked on any type of knitting as long as there are chain selvedges on the pieces to be joined.

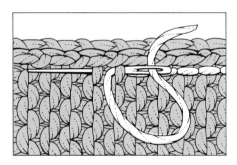

Place the right sides of the work together and make sure that the edges are absolutely level. Keep your line of stitches as straight as possible and try to ensure that the stitches are of uniform length. Working from right to left and from back to front, insert the needle through the first pair of stitches, looping the yarn around the end of the seam. Insert the needle, again from back to front, through the second pair of stitches, pull the yarn through and insert the needle, from front to back, in the previous pair of stitches then, from back to front, in the following two stitches. The stitches on the back of your work will be twice as long as those on the front.

Slip stitch

One of the neatest ways of fastening double neckbands down or of attaching a pocket is to use slip stitch. Always use the line of the stitches as a guide to stop the work twisting. When you are folding a neckband on itself, the stitch through which each slip stitch is made must be in the same vertical row as the cast-off stitch to which it is to be fastened. Slip stitch can also be used to fasten down a neckband on which the stitches have not been cast off but have been held on a thread. As each slip stitch is made through the held stitch, the thread may be removed.

Flat seams

Back stitch leaves a raised seam when the garment is opened out, and it is, therefore, most suitable for fairly lightweight yarns. If you have used a heavy yarn and when you are attaching buttonbands or collars, use a flat seam to give a neat finish on the right side of the completed garment. With right sides together and using a blunt tapestry needle, insert the needle through the edge stitch on the back piece of work and through the edge stitch of the front piece of work, pulling the yarn firmly through to the front. Repeat the process, making sure that you always sew through the stitches on the edge of your work, not through the loops between stitches.

Knitting seams together

When shoulders have not been shaped or have been shaped by turning (rather than by casting off), knitting the seams together provides a neat, flat join. It is, of course, essential that the two pieces of work to be joined in this way have exactly the same number of stitches, and no matter how carefully you have followed the pattern, always double check the number of stitches held before beginning to work this type of seam. Hold the two pieces to be joined, right sides together, on their respective needles in your left hand. Hold a slightly larger gauge needle in your right hand and put the point of the right-hand needle through the front of the first stitch on the front needle and then through the front of the first stitch on the back needle. Make a normal knit stitch, pulling a loop through both stitches to make one stitch on the right-hand needle and slipping the two stitches off the left-hand needles. Work in this way until there are two stitches on the right-hand needle, then lift the second stitch over the first, as you would if you were casting off normally. Although holding and working with two needles in the left hand can seem awkward at first, this technique is well worth mastering as it creates a strong, neat seam on the right side of the work. It can also be used, with wrong sides together, to create a decorative ridge on the finished garment.

SWISS DARNING

Swiss darning is a type of embroidery used on knitted fabrics to create a pattern that appears to be knitted in. It is worked on stocking stitch with a yarn that is of the same weight to that of the piece of knitting.

Thread a blunt darning needle with the yarn. Insert the needle from back to front of the work at the centre of the first stitch to be embroidered over, taking care not to split the knitted stitches. Insert the needle behind both threads of the stitch above, then through the next two strands below. Take care to keep the tension of the embroidered stitches the same as that of the knitting so that your work does not pucker. If the embroidery is to cover several rows, complete one row as described above, and insert the needle under the upper loop of the last stitch. Turn the work upside down and embroider across the next row.

In addition to being worked vertically and horizontally, Swiss darning is also often used to create diagonal patterns.

SUBSTITUTE YARNS AVAILABLE IN THE US:

Melinda Coss mohair	Wendy Mohair '90
Melinda Coss tussah silk	Anny Blatt Silk Anny or Rowan Silkstones
Melinda Coss DK wool	Wendy DK Merino
Melinda Coss fine chenille	Rowan fine cotton chenille
Melinda Coss DK cotton	Rowan handknit DK cotton
Melinda Coss cotton bouclé mix	Wendy Capri
Melinda Coss angora	Anny Blatt Angora Super
Melinda Coss 6-ply mercerized cotton	Anny Blatt Coton Egypte 2
Melinda Coss Aran Wool	Rowan Magpie or Wendy Kintyre
Melinda Coss chunky chenille	Rowan cotton chenillo
Melinda Coss 4-ply wool	Rowan Botany 4-ply
Melinda Coss alpaca	Wendy DK Merino
Melinda Coss chunky	Rowan Magpie (used double)

SUPPLIERS:

Wendy Wools, Berroco Inc, Elmdale Road, PO Box 367, Uxbridge, Massachussetts 01569.
Rowan Yarns, Westminster Trading, 5 Northern Boulevard, Amherst, NH 03031.
Laines Anny Blatt, 24752 Crestview Court, Farmington Hills, MI 48335.

ABBREVIATIONS

alt = alternate
beg = beginning
c4b = cable 4 back – i.e., slip first 2 stitches on to a cable needle and hold at back of work, knit second 2 stitches, knit 2 stitches from cable needle
c4f = cable 4 forwards – i.e., slip first 2 stitches on to a cable needle and hold at front of work, knit second 2 stitches, knit 2 stitches from cable needle
c6b = cable 6 back – i.e., slip first 3 stitches on to a cable needle and hold at back of work, knit second 3 stitches, knit 3 stitches from cable needle
c6f = cable 6 forward; as c6b, but hold stitches at front of work
c8b = cable 8 back; as c6b, but work over 8 stitches
c8f = cable 8 forwards; as c6f, but work over 8 stitches
cont = continue
dec = decrease
foll = following
garter st = knit every row
inc = increase
k = knit
m1 = make 1 – i.e., pick up loop between 2 stitches and knit
MB = make bobble – i.e., knit 5 stitches from 1, turn, purl 5, turn, knit 2 stitches together (k2tog), knit 1, k2tog, turn, slip 1, purl 2 stitches together

(p2tog), pass slipped stitch over
moss = knit 1, purl 1 (k1, p1) to end of row; on return row purl the knit stitches and knit the purl stitches
p = purl
patt = pattern
psso = slip 1, knit 1, pass slipped stitch over
rem = remaining
rep = repeat
RS = right side
sl = slip
st(s) = stitch(es)
st st = stocking stitch
tbl = through back loop
tog = together
twist 2 = knit into second stitch on left-hand needle but, instead of slipping it off the needle, knit into the first stitch and then slip both stitches off the left-hand needle
WS = wrong side
yo = yarn over – i.e., on knit rows carry yarn over right needle to the back, thus forming an extra stitch; on purl rows work as for knit rows, but bring yarn back to the front under the right-hand needle so that it is ready for a purl stitch
yrn = yarn round needle

YARN INFORMATION

All the sample garments illustrated in this book were knitted in Melinda Coss yarns. As many of the designs use small quantities of several different colours, Melinda Coss offers individual kits containing only the quantities of yarn necessary to complete each garment. In addition, buttons, embroidery threads and trimmings are included where appropriate. Contact Melinda at 1 Copenhagen Street, London N1 0JB (telephone 071-833 3929).

For those who wish to substitute different yarns, weights are given throughout to the nearest 25gm ball. To obtain the best results, you must ensure that the tension recommended on your selected yarn matches the tension given in the pattern. Results cannot be guaranteed unless this is done.

Knitters with pattern queries are welcome to telephone the shop number above for advice.

NEEDLE CONVERSIONS

UK and Australia	USA
2	00
$2^3/_4$	1
$3^1/_4$	3

UK and Australia	USA
$3^3/_4$	4
4	5
$4^1/_2$	6
5	7
$5^1/_2$	8
$6^1/_2$	10

US TERMINOLOGY

Most knitting terms used in the UK are identical with those used by knitters in the USA. Of the exceptions, the four used in this book are listed below (UK term first).

stocking stitch (st st) = stockinette stitch
yarn round needle (yrn) = yarn over needle
cast off = bind off
tension = gauge

All the patterns have been knitted up and checked using the yarns quoted in the instructions for each garment. When you use an equivalent yarn in weight, texture and appearance, it is doubly important that you check the gauge specified for the garment.

ABORIGINE JACKET

THE INSPIRATION for this cropped, tweedy mohair jacket came from a series of Australian Aborigine bark paintings. The background is knitted in two-colour slip stitch, and each motif is worked individually, using the Fair Isle technique to give a raised effect. The one-size jacket will fit up to 96–102cm (38–40in) bust size.

Materials
Melinda Coss mohair – 300gm black (A); 175gm ecru (B); 150gm rust; 50gm mustard. 4 buttons, 2.5cm in diameter.

Needles
One pair of 5mm needles; one pair of 5½mm needles.

Tension
Using 5½mm needles and measured over slip stitch pattern, 16 sts and 20 rows = 10cm square.

Slip stitch pattern
All blank areas of the charts should be worked in two-colour (black and ecru) slip stich as follows.
Row 1: A, knit.
Row 2: A, purl.
Row 3: B, k1,* keep yarn at back and sl1 purlwise, k1. Rep from * to end.
Row 4: B, k1,* yarn forward, sl1 purlwise, yarn back, k1. Rep from * to end.
These 4 rows make up the background pattern, and they should be worked on all blank areas of the charts.

Where the symbol on the chart indicates, make a bobble (MB) in ecru as follows: k5 from 1 st, turn, p5, turn, k2tog, k1, k2tog, turn, sl1, p2tog, pass sl st over.
Use separate balls of yarn for each motif but work the motifs themselves using the Fair Isle technique.

BACK

With 5mm needles and A, cast on 118 sts. Work in k2, p2 rib for 10cm, inc 1 st at centre of last row of rib (119 sts). Change to 5½mm needles and work as follows.

Row 1: A, knit.

Row 2: A, purl. Begin to work chart as follows.

Row 3: k15A, change to B, k1,* with yarn at back, sl1 purlwise, k1. Rep from * to last 19 sts, k19A.

Row 4: p19A, change to B, k1, *yarn forward, sl1 purlwise, yarn back. Rep from * to last 15 sts, p15A.

This sets the pattern. Cont following the chart, working motifs in st st, until it is complete. Cast off all sts.

Key

☐ = 2-colour sl st (see pattern)

• = black (A)

O = ecru (B)

☒ = rust

╱ = mustard

◎ = make bobble (MB) in ecru

BACK

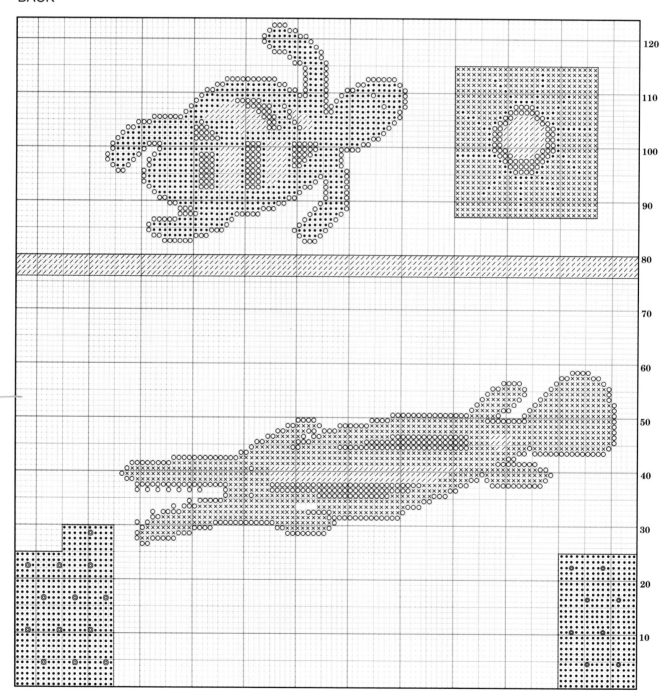

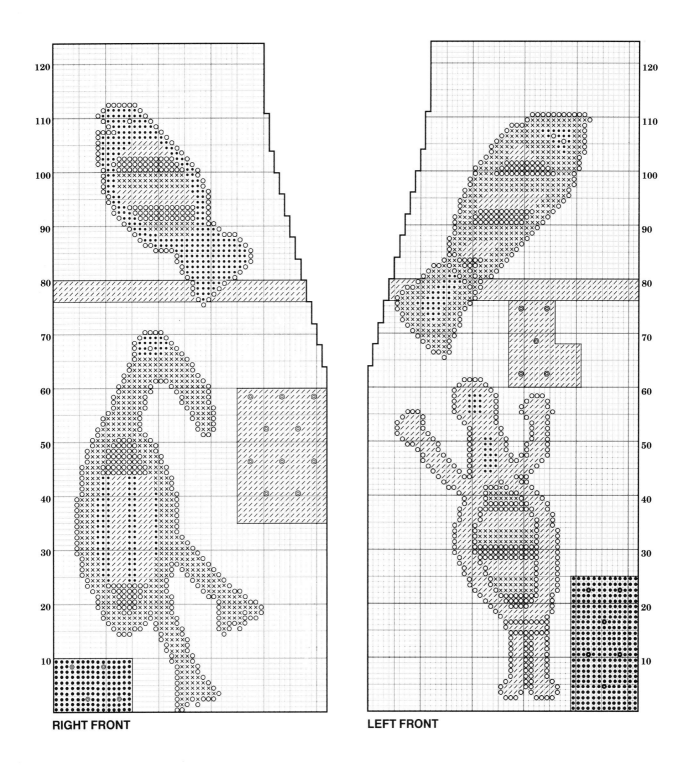

RIGHT FRONT

LEFT FRONT

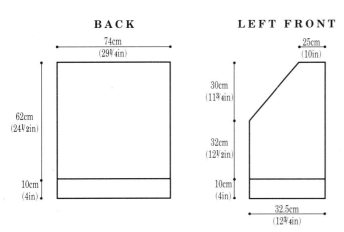

BACK

74cm
(29¼in)

62cm
(24½in)

10cm
(4in)

LEFT FRONT

25cm
(10in)

30cm
(11¾in)

32cm
(12½in)

10cm
(4in)

32.5cm
(12¾in)

LEFT FRONT

With 5mm needles and A, cast on 50 sts. Work in k2, p2 rib for 10cm, inc 1 st at the beg and end of last row of rib (52 sts). Change to 5½mm needles and begin to foll chart, working motifs in st st and the background in black and ecru sl st as for back. Work to neck shaping. RS: work patt to last 2 sts, k2tog, dec 1 st at same edge on the next 10 fourth rows and on the following seventh row. Work straight until chart is complete and cast off remaining 40 sts.

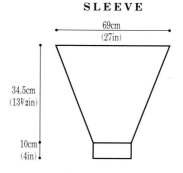

SLEEVE

69cm
(27in)

34.5cm
(13½in)

10cm
(4in)

RIGHT FRONT

Work as for left front, following chart for right front and reversing shaping.

SLEEVES

(Both alike) With 5mm needles and A, cast on 42 sts. Work 10cm in k2, p2 rib. Change to 5½mm needles and begin to foll sleeve chart, working in black and ecru sl st pattern as for back, inc 1 st each end of every alt row until you have 110 sts. Work 1 row and cast off loosely.

BUTTONBANDS AND COLLAR

Join shoulder seams. With 5½mm needles and rust, cast on 18 sts. Work in k1, p1 rib until band fits neatly to beginning of neck shaping, ending with a WS row.
Next row: rib 2, (k1, p1, k1) into next st, rib to end. Rib 3 rows. Rep the last 4 rows 11 times more, then work straight until buttonband reaches centre back neck. Cast off loosely ribwise. With pins, mark positions for 4 buttons, the first 10cm up from cast-on edge, the fourth at the beg of the neck shaping and the others spaced evenly between them.

BUTTONHOLE BAND

Work as for buttonband but make buttonholes to correspond with pins as follows. First buttonhole row (RS): rib 7 sts, cast off 4 st, rib to end. Next row: rib, casting on 4 sts over cast-off sts on previous row. Reverse shapings on collar.

MAKING UP

Using an invisible seam, join the centre back seam on the collar. Sew in the sleeves, and join the sleeve and side seams.

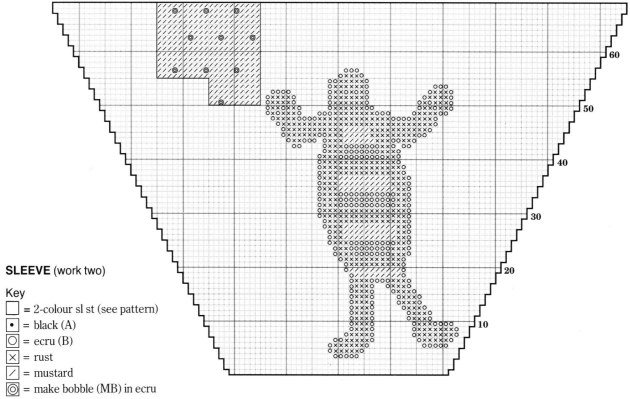

SLEEVE (work two)

Key

☐ = 2-colour sl st (see pattern)
▣ (•) = black (A)
▣ (O) = ecru (B)
▣ (×) = rust
▣ (/) = mustard
◎ = make bobble (MB) in ecru

16 · ABORIGINE JACKET

BEDOUIN TUNIC

THE RICH, BOLD STRIPES of bedouin tents provided
the inspiration for this shaped tunic top with mock
bolero. Worked in stocking stitch to a simple chart,
the one-size tunic will fit 86cm (34in) bust size. It is
knitted in tussah silk in a selection of glowing
colours.

Materials

Melinda Coss tussah silk – 275gm orange (M); 50gm
each of gold (A), red (B), lilac (C), grey (D) and
fuchsia (E).

Needles

One pair of $3^{1}/_{4}$mm needles.

Tension

Using $3^{1}/_{4}$mm needles and measured over st st, 22
sts and 32 rows = 10cm square.

N.B. X on chart and in pattern indicates garter stitch
in fuchsia

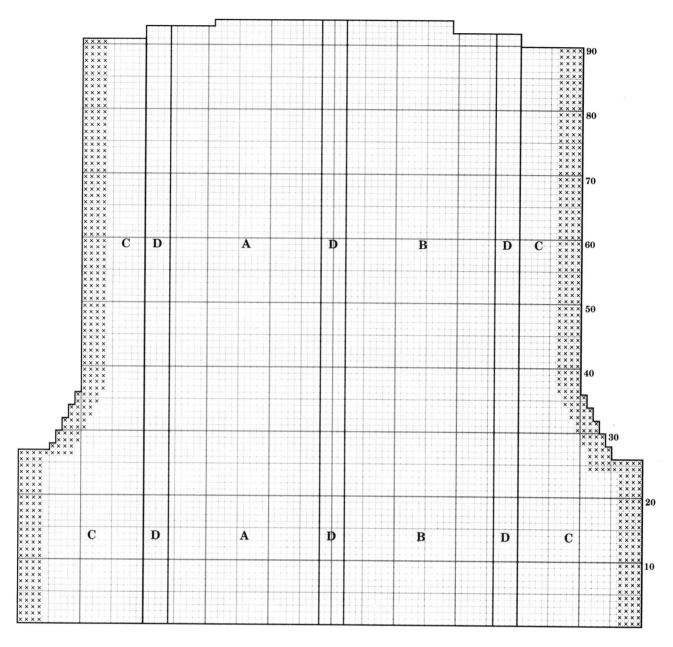

BACK

With 3¹/₄mm needles and fuchsia, cast on 108 sts and
k 2 rows. Now work stripe border section, setting
sts as follows.

Row 1 (RS): k2D, k24B, k4D, k22A, k4D, k22C,
k4D, k24B, k2D.

Row 2: p2D, p24B, p4D, p22C, p4D, p22A, p4D,
p24B, p2D.

Rep these 2 rows until work measures 4cm, ending
after a row 2, knit 4 rows in fuchsia. Break off fuchsia
and work in st st in orange for 16 rows, then start
dart shaping as follows:

Next row: k39, sl1, k1, psso, k26, k2tog, k39.

Next row: purl.

Next row: k38, sl1, k1, psso, k26, k2tog, k38.

Next row: purl.

Cont dec in this way (working 1 st fewer at each end
of row, the centre sts remaining the same
throughout), until row k21, sl1, k1, psso, k26,

Key

X	= garter st in fuchsia	C	= lilac
A	= gold	D	= grey
B	= red		

BACK

36cm
(14in)

20.5cm
(8in)

45.5cm
(18in)

46.5cm
(18¹/₂in)

49cm
(19¹/₄in)

Row 2: k4X, p16C, p4D, p24A, p4D, p24B, p4D, p16C, k4X.

Keeping chart correct and working extra sts in fuchsia as indicated, cont until row 26 has been completed.

Row 27: cast off 5, k3X (4 sts on needle), k in patt to last 9 sts, k9X.

Row 28: cast off 5 sts, k3X (4 sts on needle), p in patt to last 4 sts, k4X.

Now cont from chart, working **armhole shapings** as indicated until 80 sts rem and keeping fuchsia garter st border correct. Cont until row 90 has been completed.

Row 91: cast off 10 sts, k in patt to last 4 sts, k4X.

Row 92: cast off 10 sts, p in patt to end.

Row 93: cast off 11 sts, k in patt to end.

Row 94: cast off 11 sts, p in patt to end.

Leave rem 38 sts on a holder for back neck.

FRONT

Work as for back until work measures 37cm, ending with RS facing. Knit 2 rows in fuchsia. Now work from front chart, setting sts as follows.

Row 1: k4X, k18C, k4D, k17B, k4E, k6M, k4E, k17A, k4D, k18C, k4X.

Row 2: k4X, p18C, p4D, p17A, p4E, p6M, p4E, p17B, p4D, p18C, k4X.

With sts thus set, cont from front chart, working **armhole shapings** as indicated. Cont straight after armhole shapings have been completed.

Row 75: k4X, k8C, k4D, k15B, turn, k to end. Work on these sts for first side of front neck as follows.

Dec 1 st at neck edge on every row 8 times, then at this same edge on every alt row until 21 sts rem, then cont straight until row 90 from chart has been completed.

Row 91: cast off 10 sts, k to end.

Work 1 row, then cast off rem 11 sts. Slip centre 18 sts on to a holder for neckband, rejoin yarn to rem sts and, keeping chart correct, work to match the first side.

SLEEVES

(Both alike) With 3¼mm needles and fuchsia, cast on 40 sts and work in garter st for 2.5cm, inc into every st on last row (80 sts). Break off fuchsia, join in orange and work row of holes for draw thread as follows.

Next row: k2, *k2tog, yrn, k4. Rep from * to last st.

Now p 1 row, inc 18 sts evenly across row (98 sts). Starting with a k row, work in st st until sleeve measures 46cm, ending with RS facing.

Shape top: cast off 5 sts at beg of the next 2 rows, then dec 1 st at each end of every row until 70 sts rem, then on every row cast off 3 sts at beg of the row and dec 1 st at end of row until 38 sts rem.

Next row: k1, (k3tog) 12 times, k1.

Next row: purl.

Next row: k2tog all along the row. Cast off rem sts.

k2tog, k21 has been worked. Cont with a purl row and work in st st until back measures 24cm from cast-on edge, ending with RS facing.

Next row: k22, m1, k26, m1, k22.

Next row: purl.

Next row: k23, m1, k26, m1, k23.

Next row: purl.

Cont in this way, inc 1 st each side of centre 26 sts on every RS row, until there are 100 sts. Then cont straight until work measures 37cm, ending with RS facing. Join in fuchsia and knit 2 rows. Now work from back chart as follows.

Row 1: k4X, k16C, k4D, k24B, k4D, k24A, k4D, k16C, k4X.

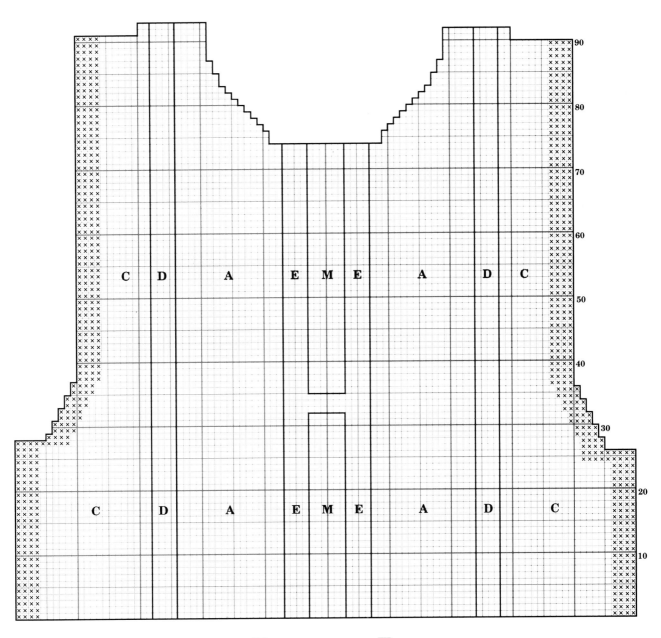

FRONT

Key

$\boxed{X}$ = garter st in fuchsia	$\boxed{B}$ = red
$\boxed{A}$ = gold	$\boxed{C}$ = lilac
	$\boxed{D}$ = grey
$\boxed{E}$ = fuchsia	
$\boxed{M}$ = orange	

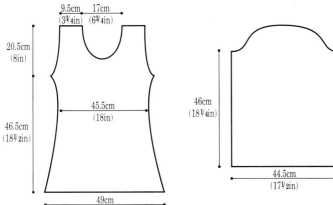

FRONT

9.5cm (3¾in)   17cm (6¾in)

20.5cm (8in)

45.5cm (18in)

46.5cm (18½in)

49cm (19¼in)

SLEEVE

46cm (18¼in)

44.5cm (17½in)

NECKBAND

Join right shoulder seam. With 3¼mm needles and RSs facing, pick up and k approx 18 sts up left front neck, the centre front neck sts, approx 18 sts up right front neck and 38 sts across back neck. Break off orange and work in garter st in fuchsia for 1.5cm. Cast off loosely.

MAKING UP

Neatly sew in all ends. Join left shoulder and neckband seams, in correct colours. Set sleeves into place, easing all fullness to top, sew into position. In correct colours, sew the side and sleeve seams. Make a draw thread to go through the holes on the sleeves, draw up and finish with a bow at the desired width.

BYZANTINE SWEATER

IN AD 330 CONSTANTINOPLE became the headquarters of the Roman Empire. Mosaics were extensively used in the architecture, art and costume of the time, and they have provided the inspiration for this simply worked, DK wool jumper, which is given in one size, suitable for up to 96cm (38in) bust.

Materials

Melinda Coss DK wool – 375gm jade (A); 100gm purple (B); 100gm mustard (C); 75gm blue (D).

Needles

One pair of 4mm needles; one pair off 3$^{1}/_{4}$mm needles; one short 3$^{1}/_{4}$mm circular needle. Stitch holders.

Tension

Using 4mm needles and measured over st st, 21 sts and 27 rows = 10cm square.

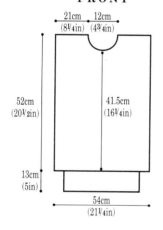

FRONT

21cm (8$^{1}/_{4}$in) — 12cm (4$^{3}/_{4}$in)

52cm (20$^{1}/_{2}$in)   41.5cm (16$^{1}/_{4}$in)

13cm (5in)

54cm (21$^{1}/_{4}$in)

FRONT

With 3$^{1}/_{4}$mm needles and A, cast on 100 sts. Begin to foll chart for front, setting rib as follows:
Row 1: p1A, k2A, p2A, k10C, *(p2A, k2A twice), p2A, k10C. Rep from * 3 times, p2A, k2A, p1A.
Row 2: k1A, p2A, k2A, *p10C, k2A, (p2A, k2A twice). Rep from * 3 times, p10C, k2A, p2A, k1A.
Cont to foll chart, working rib as set until 34 rows have been worked. Work 1 more row in rib, inc 14 sts evenly across it (114 sts). Change to 4mm needles and, starting with a k row, cont to foll chart in st st to **neck shaping.**
Next row (RS): k 51 sts in patt. Slip rem 63 sts on to a spare needle and, working on the first set of sts only, dec 1 st at neck edge on every alt row 6 times (45 sts). Work straight until chart is complete. Cast off. Return to sts held, slip centre 12 sts on to a holder, rejoin yarn to rem sts and shape neck to match other side. Cast off.

BACK

Work as for front but cont to foll chart to back neck shaping.
Next row: work patt for 45 sts, leave rem sts on a spare needle. Working on first set of sts only, complete chart then cast off loosely. Slip centre 24 sts on to a holder, rejoin yarn, complete second side of chart. Cast off.

BACK

21cm (8$^{1}/_{4}$in) — 12cm (4$^{3}/_{4}$in)

52cm (20$^{1}/_{2}$in)

13cm (5in)

54cm (21$^{1}/_{4}$in)

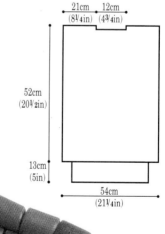

BACK AND FRONT   The dotted line indicates the back neck shaping

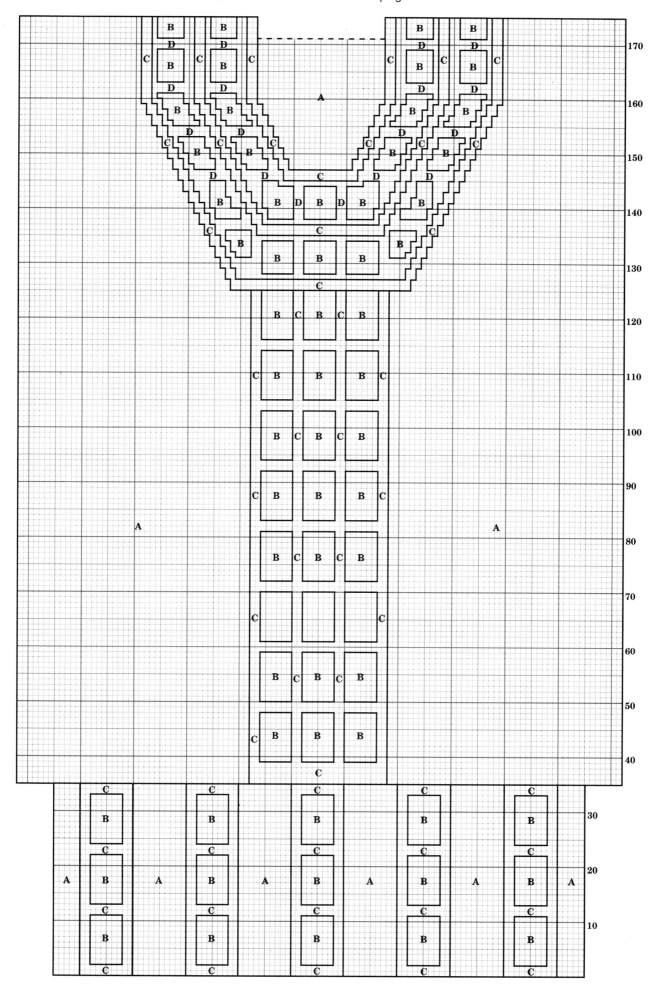

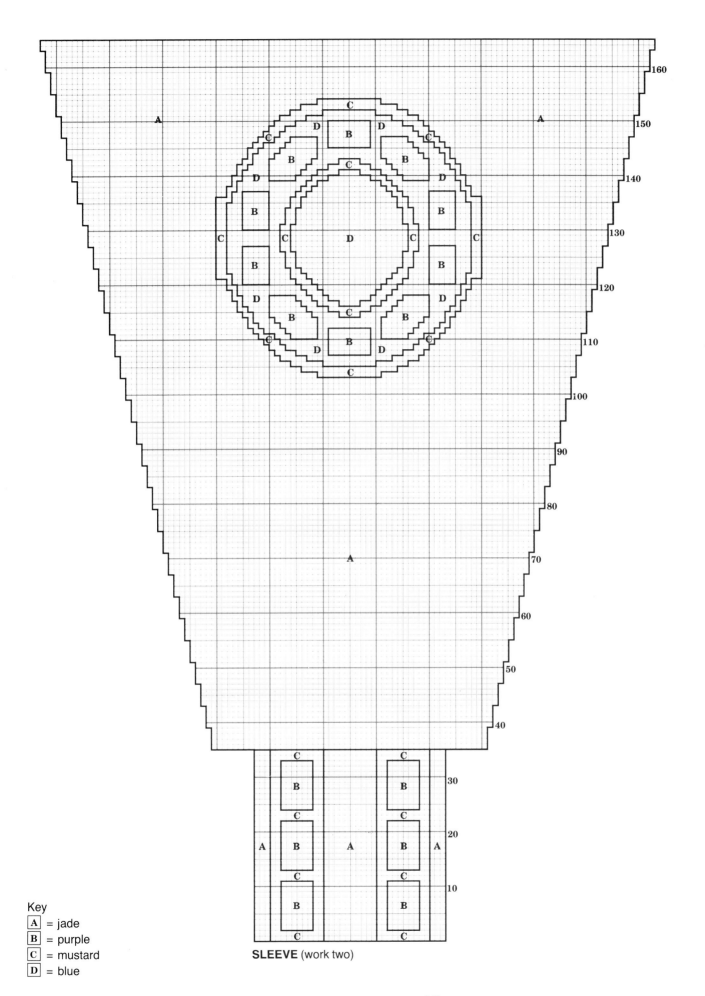

Key
A = jade
B = purple
C = mustard
D = blue

SLEEVE (work two)

SLEEVES

(Both alike) With 3¹/₄mm needles and A, cast on 36 sts. Begin following chart for sleeves, setting rib as follows.

Row 1: k1A, p2A, k10C, (p2A, k2A twice), p2A, k10C, p2A, k1A.

Row 2: p1A, k2A, p10C, k2A, (p2A, k2A twice), p10C, k2A, p1A.

Cont working in rib, following chart as set until 34 rows have been worked. Work 1 more row in rib, inc 16 sts evenly across it (52 sts). Change to 4mm needles and begin foll chart in st st, inc 1 st each end of the fifth, then every following fourth row until you have 116 sts. Complete chart. Cast off loosely. Join shoulder seams.

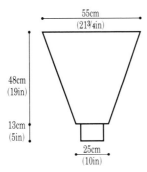

55cm
(21³/₄in)

48cm
(19in)

13cm
(5in)

25cm
(10in)

NECKBAND

With a 3¹/₄mm circular needle and B, pick up and knit 26 sts down left front neck, 12 sts from centre front, 26 sts up right front neck, 4 sts down right back, 24 sts held for centre back, 4 sts down left back (96 sts). Work 8 rows in k2, p2 rib. Cast off loosely.

MAKING UP

Join sleeves to jumper. Join side and sleeve seams.

MAN'S CHILKAT SWEATER

A CHILKAT BLANKET, worn by chiefs of the Haida Indians on the Queen Charlotte Islands, Canada, inspired the bold abstract pattern of this man's shawl-collared sweater. The cabled sweater is worked in DK wool, using the intarsia method, and will fit up to 112cm (44in) chest.

Materials

Melinda Coss DK wool – 575gm grey; 75gm mustard; 75gm black; Melinda Coss fine chenille – 100gm cream.

Needles

One pair of 4mm needles; one pair of 3¼mm needles.

Tension

Using 4mm needles and measured over st st, 24 sts and 32 rows = 10cm square.

N.B. When the X symbol appears on the chart, using grey, p on the RS of the work and k on the WS.

BACK

Using 3¼mm needles and grey, cast on 128 sts. Work in k2, p2 rib for 10cm, inc 22 sts evenly across last row of rib (150 sts). Change to 4mm needles * and, starting with a k row, begin working from chart for back. Complete the chart without shaping. Cast off all sts.

BACK

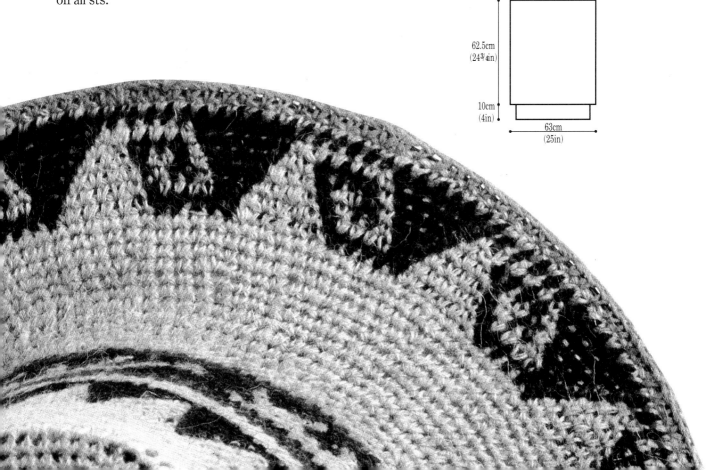

62.5cm
(24¾in)

10cm
(4in)

63cm
(25in)

BACK, FRONT AND SLEEVES

The red lines indicate the front neck shaping and the area of the chart to be worked to complete both sleeves.

Key

A = grey
Y = mustard
G = black

C = cream
⌒ = c6f in grey
☒ = k on WS and p on RS of work in grey

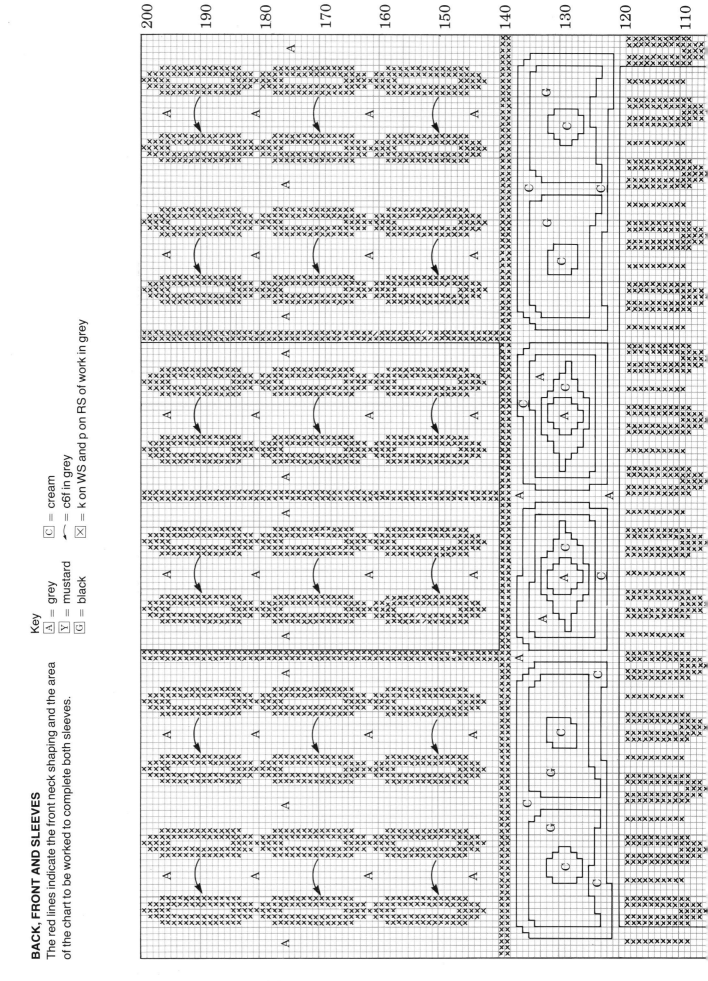

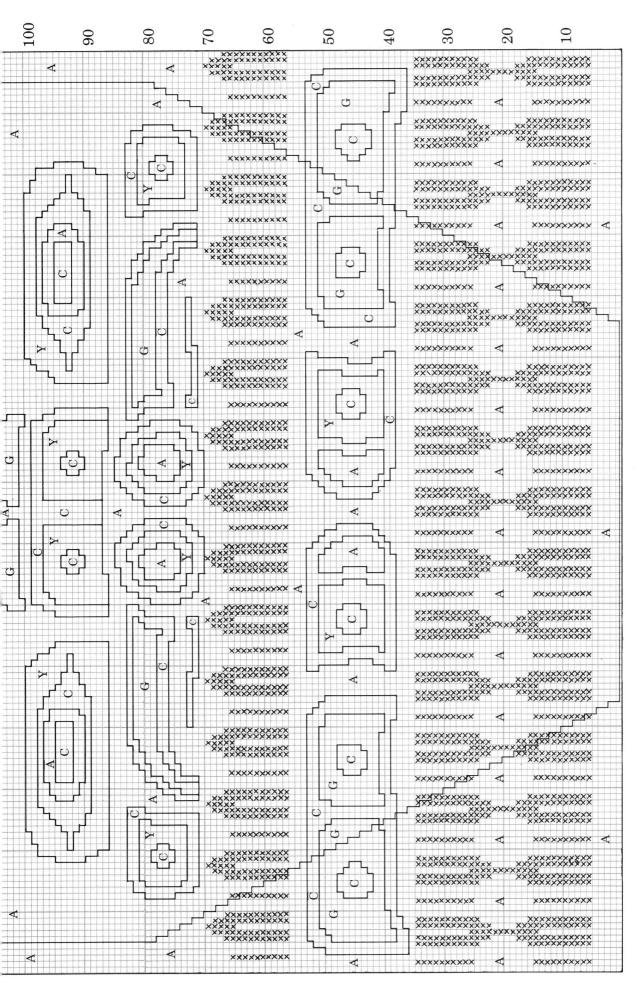

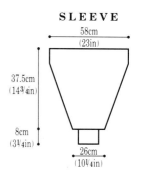

st st and inc 1 st each end of the third row and every foll alt row until you have 140 sts. Cont without further shaping until chart is complete. Cast off loosely.

Join shoulder seams.

SLEEVE

58cm
(23in)

37.5cm
(14³⁄₄in)

8cm
(3¹⁄₄in)

26cm
(10¹⁄₄in)

COLLAR

With 3¹⁄₄mm needles and grey, cast on 188 sts and work in k2, p2 rib for 16cm. Cast off loosely in rib.

MAKING UP

Pin cast-on edge of collar into position around neck, placing left side over right side at centre front. Stitch the short ends neatly into position across centre front neck (left side directly on top of right side). Join the sleeves to the body, and join the side and sleeve seams using narrow back stitch.

FRONT

Work as for back to * and, starting with a k row, begin to foll chart and work straight to **neck shaping**.

Next row (RS): work patt for 50 sts and slip these sts on to a spare needle. Cast off centre 50 sts; work patt to end. Cont working from chart on this last set of sts only until it is complete. Cast off. With WS facing, rejoin yarn to rem sts and foll chart until it is complete. Cast off.

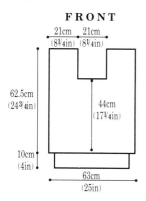

FRONT

21cm   21cm
(8¹⁄₄in)   (8¹⁄₄in)

62.5cm
(24³⁄₄in)

44cm
(17¹⁄₄in)

10cm
(4in)

63cm
(25in)

SLEEVES

(Both alike) Using 3¹⁄₄mm needles and grey, cast on 54 sts and work in k2, p2 rib for 8cm, inc 8 sts evenly across last row of rib (62 sts). Change to 4mm needles and begin to foll chart for sleeve, working in

CLEOPATRA SWEATER

EGYPTIAN TRADITIONAL DRESS is often heavily decorated with beads. Beads are knitted into the body of this sweater and sewn on to the yoke to simulate the heavy jewelled collars worn by Cleopatra. The sweater can be knitted to fit bust sizes 86/96cm (34/38in), and the motif band should be worked using the intarsia method.

Materials

Melinda Coss DK cotton – 525/550gm black; 50gm green; 50gm red; 25gm blue; 25gm white; 25gm gold. 38 round red beads; 35 round green beads, 48 tubular red beads; 24 tubular blue beads. 1 black button, 1.5cm in diameter.

Needles

One pair of 3¹/₄mm needles; one pair of 4mm needles; one 4mm circular needle, 100cm long. Stitch holders.

Tension

Using 4mm needles and measured over st st, 20 sts and 24 rows = 10cm square.

FRONT

With 3¹/₄mm needles and black, cast on 80/86 sts and work in k2, p2 rib for 2 rows. Change to red and cont in rib for 18 more rows, inc 20/24 sts evenly across last row of rib (100/110 sts). Starting with a round red bead, thread 9 red and 9 green beads alternately on to the black yarn.

Change to 4mm needles and cont to foll the chart until row 44 is complete.

Next row: k5/10, slip bead, k28, slip bead, k27, slip bead, k27, slip bead, k to end. Work 15 rows in st st. Next row (RS): k19/24, slip bead, k28, slip bead, k27, slip bead, k to end. Work 15 rows in st st. Rep first bead row. St st 15 rows. Rep second bead row. Cont straight until 104 rows have been worked from the beg of the chart.

Shape yoke first size: dec 1 st at each end of the next row and the foll alt row, p 1 row.

Next row (RS): k2tog, k2, slip bead, k28, slip bead, k27, slip bead, k27, slip bead, k to last 2 sts, k2tog.* Dec 1 st at each end of the 7 foll alt rows. At the same time, when 88 sts rem and working on a RS row, shape neck.

Shape yolk second size: dec 1 st each end of the next 4 rows.

Next row: k2tog, k5, slip bead, k28, slip bead, k27, slip bead, k27, slip bead, k to last 2 sts, k2tog.* Dec 1 st each end of the next 5 rows (88 sts).

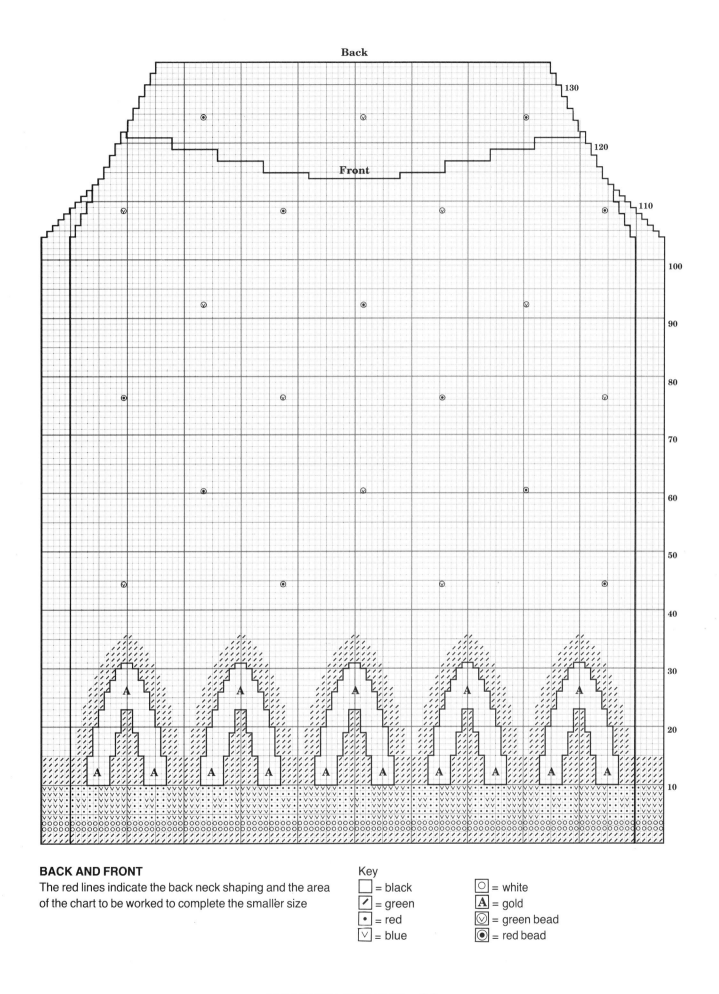

BACK AND FRONT

The red lines indicate the back neck shaping and the area
of the chart to be worked to complete the smaller size

Key

☐ = black	⊙ = white
⬧ = green	**A** = gold
• = red	⊙ = green bead
∨ = blue	⊙ = red bead

Shape neck both sizes: cont dec 1 st at each end of every alt row. Work 36 sts and place these on a st holder. Cast off 16 sts, k to last 2 sts, k2tog, p 1 row. Cast off 8 sts, k to end, p 1 row.
Rep these last 2 rows 3 times more. Secure rem st. Pick up sts on holder and shape to match first side, following chart. Secure last st.

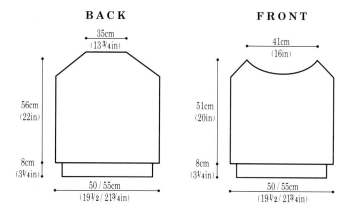

BACK   FRONT

BACK

Starting with a round red bead, slip 11 red and 10 green beads alternately on to the black yarn and work as for front to *.
First size: cont dec 1 st each end of every alt row until 78 sts rem, ending with a WS row.
Second size: dec 1 st each end of the next 6 rows, then dec 1 st each end of every alt row until 78 sts rem, ending with a WS row.
Both sizes: k2tog, k8, slip bead, k28, slip bead, k27 slip bead, k to last 2 sts, k2tog. Cont to dec 1 st at each end of every alt row until 70 sts rem. Cast off 35 sts, mark with coloured thread, cast off rem 35 sts.

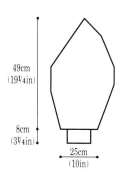

RIGHT SLEEVE

Starting with a red bead, thread 9 red and 8 green beads alternately on to black yarn. With 3^{1}/$_{4}$mm needles and black, cast on 44 sts and work 2 rows in k2, p2 rib. Change to red and work 18 more rows in k2, p2 rib, inc 6 sts evenly across the last row (50 sts). Change to 4mm needles and black, and cont in st st, slipping beads in the foll positions.
Row 11: k10, slip bead, k28, slip bead, k to end.
Row 27: k3, slip bead, k27, slip bead, k28, slip bead, k to end.

Row 43: k21, slip bead, k28, slip bead, k to end.
Row 59: k11, slip bead, k27, slip bead, k28, slip bead, k to end.
Row 75: k25, slip bead, k28, slip bead, k to end.
Row 91: k10, slip bead, k27, slip bead, k28, slip bead, k to end.
Row 107: k16, slip bead, k28, slip bead, k to end.
At the same time inc 1 st each end of the third row and the 14 foll fourth rows (80 sts). Work straight to row 90, then dec 1 st each end of the next row and the 9 foll alt rows. Work 1 row *.
Next row (RS): cast off 11 sts, work to last 2 sts, k2tog. Work 1 row. Rep the last 2 rows until 1 st rem. Secure last st.

LEFT SLEEVE

Work as for right sleeve to *, then cont as for right sleeve but reverse shapings.

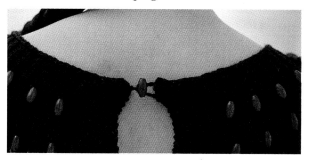

YOKE

Using 4mm circular needle and black, start at the thread marker and pick up across the RS 35 sts from centre back, 55 sts across top of left sleeve, 80 sts across front, 55 sts across right sleeve and 35 sts across back (260 sts). Work 10 sts in moss st, then k3, p2 rib to last 10 sts. Work these in moss st.
Next row: moss 10, k2, p3 to last 10 sts, moss 10.
Make back opening: rep these 2 rows 3 times more, but work from edge to edge instead of completing a full circle. Work 1 more row in patt.
Next row: moss 8, k2tog, dec 48 sts along the row on k sts so that rib becomes k2, p2, ending with k2tog, moss 8, then, continuing the moss borders, work 9 rows in k2, p2 rib.
Next row: moss 7, k2tog, dec 48 sts along row on k sts so that rib becomes k2, p1, ending with a k2tog, moss 7. Cont in k2, p1 for 9 rows.
Next row: change to 3^{1}/$_{4}$mm needles, moss 6, k2tog, dec 48 sts along row on k sts so that rib becomes k1, p1. Work in k1, p1 rib for 7 rows.
Next row: moss 5, k2tog, k1, p1 rib to last 7 sts, k2tog, moss 5. Work 1 more row, then cast off loosely, knitwise over rib and ribwise over moss.

MAKING UP

Join the underarm and side seams using a flat seam. Make a small chain loop at the top of the moss stitch back opening and sew the button in position on other side. Sew tubular beads on the yoke to form a collar, using the photograph as a guide.

ESKIMO JACKET

THE DESIGN FOR THE BORDER of this mohair jacket
was inspired by the textiles of the Dene Indians of
northwestern Canada. The jacket is quoted in one
size, which will fit up to 96cm (38in) bust.

Materials
Melinda Coss mohair – 400gm bright blue; 200gm
crimson; 100gm turquoise; 50gm gold; 50gm scarlet.

Needles
One pair of 5mm needles; one pair of $5^{1}/_{2}$mm
needles; one 5mm circular needle, 80cm long.

Tension
Using $5^{1}/_{2}$mm needles and measured over st st, 16
sts and 21 rows = 10cm square.

BACK
With 5mm needles and crimson, cast on 117 sts.
Work in k2, p2 rib for 10cm, inc 1 st at the centre of
the last row (118 sts). Change to $5^{1}/_{2}$mm needles and
blue, work 2 rows in st st.
Next row: begin to foll chart for back as follows.
Work first row until it is complete, then work from
stitch 10 to end, then repeat from stitch 10 to end of
row. Work 30 rows of chart in st st. Cont in blue only
until back measures 72cm. Cast off loosely.

BACK

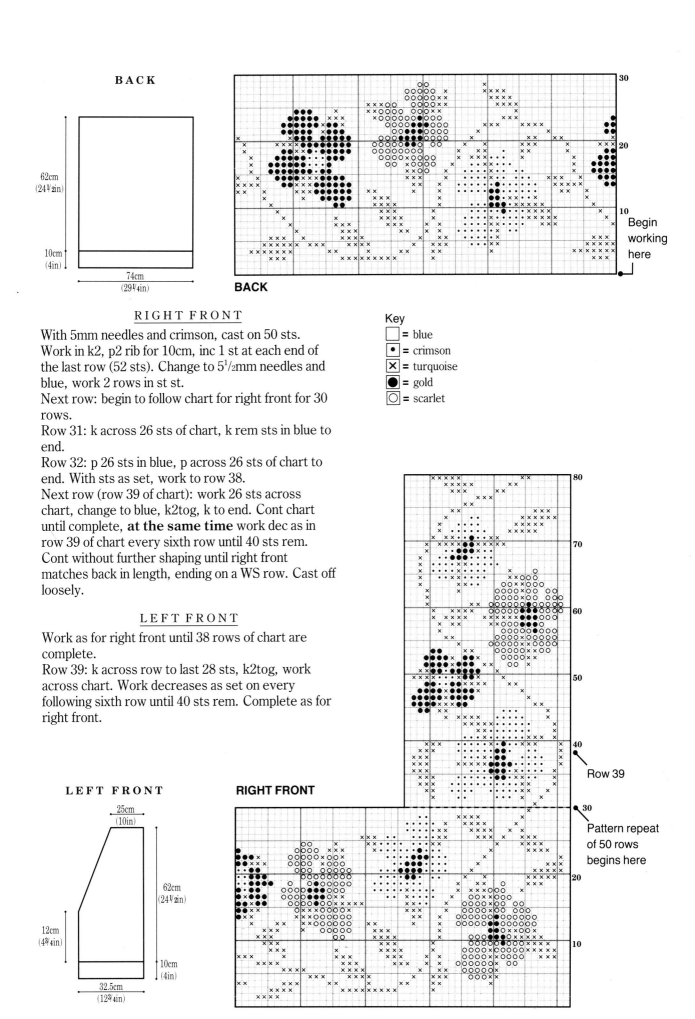

BACK

RIGHT FRONT

With 5mm needles and crimson, cast on 50 sts.
Work in k2, p2 rib for 10cm, inc 1 st at each end of
the last row (52 sts). Change to $5^1/2$mm needles and
blue, work 2 rows in st st.
Next row: begin to follow chart for right front for 30
rows.
Row 31: k across 26 sts of chart, k rem sts in blue to
end.
Row 32: p 26 sts in blue, p across 26 sts of chart to
end. With sts as set, work to row 38.
Next row (row 39 of chart): work 26 sts across
chart, change to blue, k2tog, k to end. Cont chart
until complete, **at the same time** work dec as in
row 39 of chart every sixth row until 40 sts rem.
Cont without further shaping until right front
matches back in length, ending on a WS row. Cast off
loosely.

LEFT FRONT

Work as for right front until 38 rows of chart are
complete.
Row 39: k across row to last 28 sts, k2tog, work
across chart. Work decreases as set on every
following sixth row until 40 sts rem. Complete as for
right front.

Key

☐ = blue
⊡ = crimson
☒ = turquoise
⬤ = gold
○ = scarlet

LEFT FRONT

RIGHT FRONT

Row 39

Pattern repeat
of 50 rows
begins here

SLEEVE

69cm
(27in)

38cm
(15in)

10cm
(4in)

26cm
(10¼in)

SLEEVES

(Both alike) With 5mm needles and crimson, cast on 42 sts. Work in k2, p2 rib for 10cm. Change to 5½mm needles and blue. Inc 1 st each end of next and every foll alt row until you have 110 sts and sleeve measures 48cm ending on a WS row. Cast off loosely.

FRONT BANDS AND COLLAR

Join shoulder seams. With RSs facing, using a 5mm circular needle and crimson, knit up 78 sts up right front, to beg of shaping, 57 sts up to shoulder, 48 sts across back neck, 57 sts down to beg of shaping and 78 sts down to cast-on edge (318 sts). Beg with p2, work 17 rows in k2, p2 rib.

Shape collar: rib 240, turn, rib 162, turn, rib 158, turn, rib 154, turn, rib 150, turn, rib 146, turn, and cont this way until rib 130, turn has been worked. Rib 134, turn, rib 138, turn, rib 142, turn, rib 146, turn, and cont in this way until rib 162, turn has been worked. Rib 240, turn, rib to end (318 sts). Work 18 rows in k2, p2 rib. Cast off loosely ribwise.

MAKING UP

Join the sleeves to the jacket using narrow back stitch. Join the side and sleeve seams. Fold the collar and front bands in half to WS and stitch down. Finally, complete the flower on both shoulder seams by Swiss darning with scarlet the rest of the flower, using the chart as your guide.

LEFT FRONT

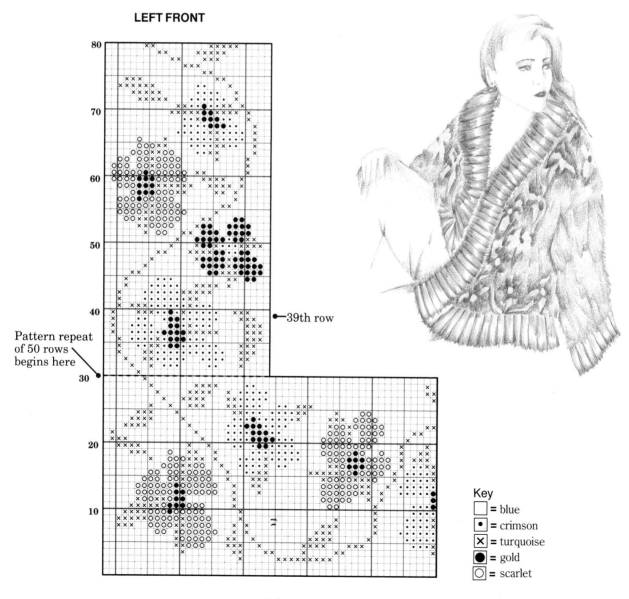

Pattern repeat
of 50 rows
begins here

39th row

Key

□ = blue
• = crimson
☒ = turquoise
● = gold
○ = scarlet

JACKET FROM GHANA

THE TRADITIONAL MOTIFS used on this design were first adopted for a modern woven silk and cotton hammock that originated among the Ewe people of Ghana. The pattern is converted here into DK wool, and the unusual combination of colour and texture emphasizes the rich patterning. The one-size jacket will fit up to 92cm (36in) bust.

Materials

Melinda Coss DK wool – 325gm burnt sienna; 125gm yellow; 125gm ecru; 100gm blue; 50gm green; 50gm mauve; 25gm black; 25gm red. 8 buttons, 2cm in diameter.

Needles

One pair of 3$^{1}/_{4}$mm needles; one pair of 4mm needles. Stitch holders.

Tension

Using 4mm needles and measured over st st, 24 sts and 32 rows = 10cm square.

BACK

With 3$^{1}/_{4}$mm needles and blue, cast on 120 sts. K1, p1 rib for 1 row, change to burnt sienna and cont in rib until your work measures 12cm. Change to 4mm needles and begin to foll chart, inc 1 st each end of every eighth row until there are 132 sts. Cont foll chart, working cables as indicated. When chart is complete, cast off 40 sts in yellow at the beg of the next 2 rows. Cast off rem 52 sts.

BACK

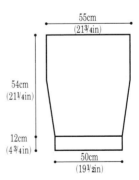

55cm
(21$^{3}/_{4}$in)

54cm
(21$^{1}/_{4}$in)

12cm
(4$^{3}/_{4}$in)

50cm
(19$^{1}/_{2}$in)

| 170 |
| 160 |
| 150 |
| 140 |
| 130 |
| 120 |
| 110 |
| 100 |
| 90 |
| 80 |
| 70 |
| 60 |
| 50 |
| 40 |
| 30 |
| 20 |
| 10 |

RIGHT FRONT **LEFT FRONT**

Key
☐ = burnt sienna ⊠ = ecru ⊡ = blue ➤— = c6b
⊙ = yellow ⬤ = black ▲ = red —◀ = c6f
⊡ = yellow ▷ = mauve ⊟ = green

BACK, LEFT AND RIGHT FRONTS AND SLEEVES
The red lines indicate the front neck shaping, the division
for the left and right fronts and the area of the chart to be
worked to complete both sleeves

LEFT/FRONT

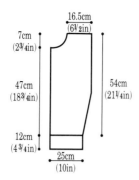

16.5cm (6½in)

7cm (2¾in)

47cm (18¾in)

54cm (21¼in)

12cm (4¾in)

25cm (10in)

SLEEVE

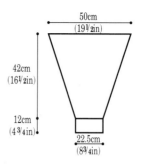

50cm (19½in)

42cm (16½in)

12cm (4¾in)

22.5cm (8¾in)

LEFT FRONT

With 3¼mm needles and blue, cast on 60 sts. Work 1 row in k1, p1 rib, change to burnt sienna and cont in rib as for back. Change to 4mm needles and work left front chart to neck shaping. With RS facing, work patt across 54 sts and turn, leaving rem sts on a holder. Working on these 54 sts only, cast off 3 sts at the beg of the next row, then 2 sts at neck edge on every alt row 3 times, then 1 st on every alt row 5 times. Work straight for 2 rows, cast off in yellow. Rejoin yarn to sts held at centre front and cast off.

RIGHT FRONT

Work as for left front to neck shaping. With RS facing, cast off 12 sts and patt to end. Work 1 row, cast off 3 sts at the beg of the next row, 2 sts at the beg of the foll 3 alt rows, then 1 st on every alt row 5 times. Work 2 rows in yellow, cast off in yellow.

SLEEVES

With 3¼mm needles and blue, cast on 54 sts. Work 1 row in k1, p1 rib, change to burnt sienna and work in rib as for back. Change to 4mm needles and work sleeve as indicated on chart, inc 1 st each end of every foll fourth row until you have 120 sts. Complete chart. Cast off loosely.

BUTTONBAND

With 3¼mm needles and blue, cast on 11 sts. Work 1 row in k1, p1 rib, change to burnt sienna and cont in rib until band fits neatly up to neck shaping when slightly stretched. Sew neatly into place up left front. Mark positions for 8 buttons, the first button 1cm from cast-on edge, the top button 1cm from cast-off edge, with the other 6 spaced evenly between them.

BUTTONHOLE BAND

Work as for buttonband, at the same time working buttonholes to correspond with buttons as follows.
Row 1: k1, p1 twice, cast off 3 sts, rib to end.
Row 2: rib 4, cast on 3, rib to end.

COLLAR

With RS facing, 3¼mm needles and burnt sienna, pick up and k 51 sts up right neck, 52 sts across back neck, 51 sts down left neck (154 sts). Work 10 rows in garter st (k every row), change to 4mm needles and cont in garter st for another 14 rows. Cast off 1 st at the beg of the next 6 rows, 2 sts at the beg of the next 4 rows, 3 sts at the beg of the next 4 rows, then 4 sts at beg of the next 4 rows. Cast off all sts.

MAKING UP

Using narrow back stitch, join the sleeves to the jumper. Sew on the buttonhole band, and join the side and sleeve seams. Sew the collar into position and sew on the buttons.

GUJARATI SWEATER

THE APPLIQUÉD TEXTILES and embroideries of western India are the inspiration behind this DK wool jumper. The motifs are knitted in and then stitched around the edges to give a 'sewn on' effect. This one-size sweater will fit up to bust size 96cm (38in).

Materials
Melinda Coss DK wool – 500gm heather; 150gm charcoal; 125gm gold; 100gm leaf green; 75gm copper; 50gm jade.

Needles
One pair of $3^3/_4$mm needles; one pair of $3^1/_4$mm needles; one short $3^1/_4$mm circular needle. Stitch holder.

Tension
Using $3^3/_4$mm needles and measured over st st, 26 sts and 30 rows = 10cm square.

BACK
With $3^1/_4$mm needles and charcoal, cast on 150 sts.
Row 1 (WS): *k2, p2, rep from * to end.
Row 2: **twist 2 (k into second st on left-hand needle but do not slip it off the needle, instead k into the first st and then slip both off the left-hand needle), p2, rep from ** to end.
Repeat the last 2 rows until rib measures 6cm.
Change to $3^3/_4$mm needles and begin to foll the chart in st st, ignoring the decorative neck border but cont straight in heather until the chart is complete. Slip all sts on to a spare needle, placing markers 52 sts in from each edge for shoulders.

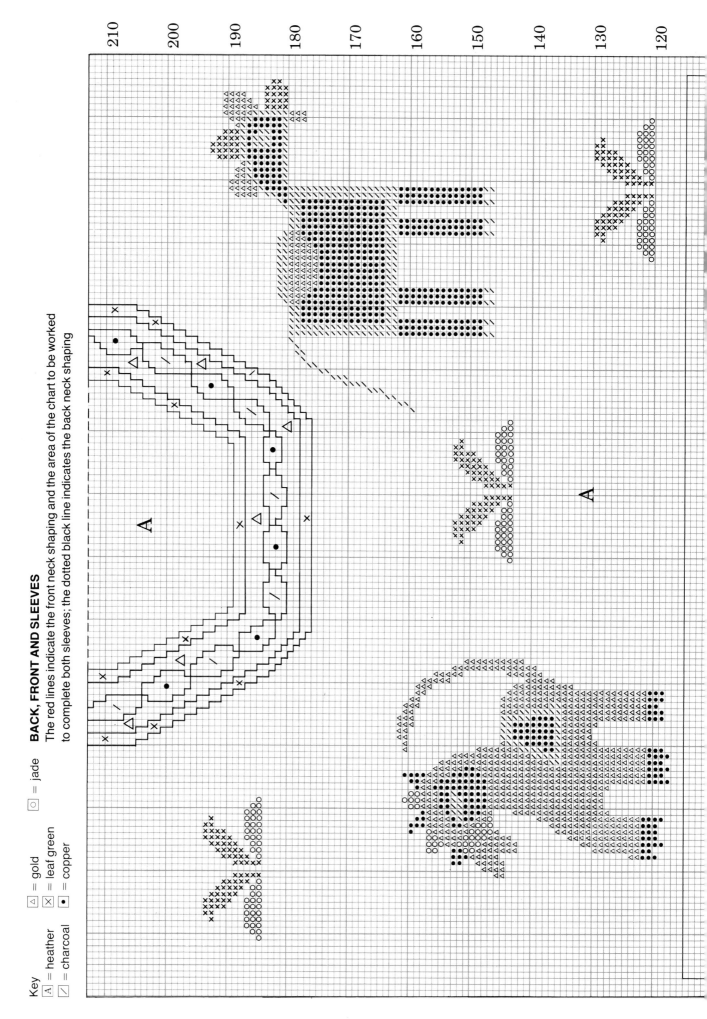

210
200
190
180
170
160
150
140
130
120

Key

△ = gold ○ = jade

× = heather

/ = leaf green • = copper

• = charcoal

BACK, FRONT AND SLEEVES

The red lines indicate the front neck shaping and the area of the chart to be worked to complete both sleeves; the dotted black line indicates the back neck shaping

BACK

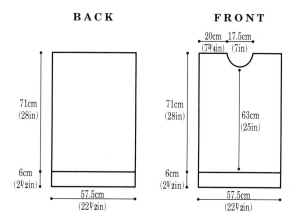

71cm
(28in)

6cm
(2¹/₂in)

57.5cm
(22¹/₂in)

FRONT

20cm   17.5cm
(7³/₄in)   (7in)

71cm
(28in)

63cm
(25in)

6cm
(2¹/₂in)

57.5cm
(22¹/₂in)

FRONT

Work as for back to neck shaping.
Next row: work 62 sts and leave rem sts on a spare needle. Working on this first set of sts only, dec 1 st at neck edge on next row and the 9 following alt rows (52 sts). Work straight until chart is complete, leave sts on a spare needle. Return to held sts and slip centre 26 sts on to a st holder. Work to end. Dec 1 st at neck edge on next row and the 9 foll alt rows. Work until chart is complete, leaving remaining 52 sts on a spare needle.

SLEEVE

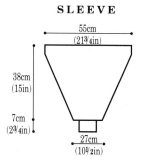

55cm
(21³/₄in)

38cm
(15in)

7cm
(2³/₄in)

27cm
(10¹/₂in)

SLEEVES

Using 3¹/₄mm needles and charcoal, cast on 50 sts.
Work in double twisted rib as for body for 7cm, inc 20 sts evenly across last row of rib (70 sts). Change

to 3³/₄mm needles and begin to foll chart for sleeve in st st, inc 1 st each end of every third row until you have 144 sts. Work 4 rows, cast off loosely.
Knit shoulder seams together.

NECKBAND

Using a 3¹/₄mm circular needle, charcoal and with RSs of work facing, pick up and k 24 sts down the left side of neck, the 26 sts held for centre front, 24 sts up the right side of neck and the 46 sts held for back (120 sts). Work in double twisted rib as for body for 5cm. Cast off loosely in rib.

MAKING UP

Using copper wool and small stitches, oversew around the animal motifs to give the impression that the motifs have been appliquéd. Join the sleeves to the jumper, and join the sleeve and side seams using flat seams throughout.

GYPSY SWEATER

Materials
Melinda Coss DK wool – 500gm red; 100gm white; 75gm royal blue; 75gm bottle green; 75gm gold; 25gm brown. 3 wooden beads for buttons.

Needles
One pair of 3¼mm needles; one pair of 4mm needles. Stitch holder.

Tension
Using 4mm needles and measured over st st, 24 sts and 32 rows = 10cm square.

THIS SWEATER was inspired by the paintings that gypsies in Europe and North America used to adorn their barges and caravans. The one-size sweater is worked in DK wool and will fit up to 96cm (38in) bust.

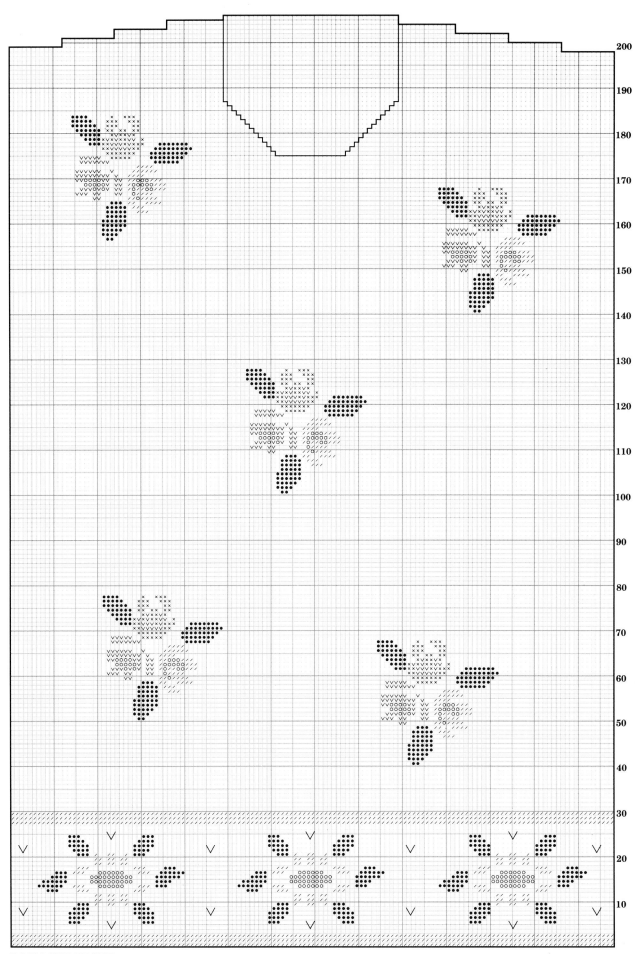

BACK AND FRONT

BACK

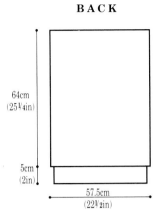

64cm
(25¼in)

5cm
(2in)

57.5cm
(22½in)

BACK

With 3¼mm needles cast on (8 sts each in blue, green, yellow and brown) 4 times, then 8 sts in blue (136 sts).

Row 1: (k1, p1 4 times in blue, k1, p1 4 times in brown, k1, p1 4 times in yellow, k1, p1 4 times in green, k1, p1 4 times in blue). Keeping in colours as set, rep across row, then cont in rib until work measures 5cm, inc 1 st at each end of the last row (138 sts).

Change to 4mm needles and, starting with a k row, work in st st from chart to shoulder shaping. Cast off 12 sts at the beg of the next 6 rows, then 13 sts at the beg of the next 2 rows. Leave remaining sts on a holder for neckband.

FRONT

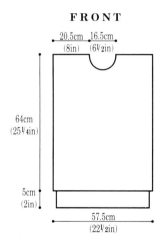

20.5cm   16.5cm
(8in)   (6½in)

64cm
(25¼in)

5cm
(2in)

57.5cm
(22½in)

FRONT

With 3¼mm needles cast on for rib: (8 sts each in brown, yellow, green and blue) 4 times, then 8 sts in brown (136 sts). Work in k1, p1 rib as set for 5cm, inc 1 st each end of the last row (138 sts).
Change to 4mm needles and work from chart to front neck shaping. **Shape neck:** work 61 sts, turn, cont following chart, working on this first set of sts only. Dec 1 st at neck edge on every row until 49 sts rem, then cont straight from chart to shoulder shaping. Cast off 12 sts at the beg of the next and foll 2 alt rows, work 1 row, cast off remaining sts. Slip centre 16 sts on to a holder for neck, rejoin yarn to remaining sts and, keeping chart correct, work to match first side.

Key

☐ = Red
⟋ = Gold
◻ = Brown
● = Green
☒ = White
⟈ = Blue

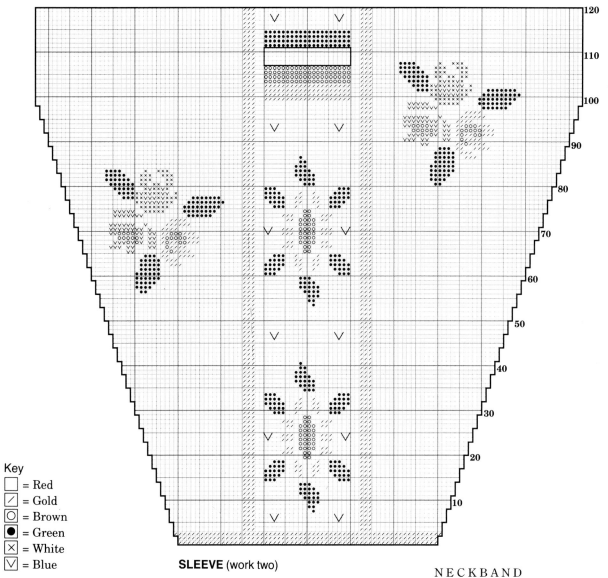

Key

☐ = Red
⟋ = Gold
◉ = Brown
● = Green
⊠ = White
⋁ = Blue

SLEEVE (work two)

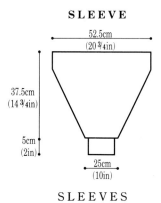

SLEEVE

52.5cm
(20 ¾in)

37.5cm
(14 ¾in)

5cm
(2in)

25cm
(10in)

SLEEVES

(Both alike) With 3¼mm needles, cast on 8 sts blue,
8 sts brown, 8 sts yellow, 8 sts green, 8 sts blue, 8
sts brown (48 sts). Work in k1, p1 rib and stripe as
for back until work measures 7.5cm, inc 2 sts across
each colour on last row (60 sts). Change to 4mm
needles and work from chart, inc 1 st at each end of
every third row until there are 126 sts. Work
without further shaping until chart is complete. Cast
off all sts.

NECKBAND

Join right shoulder seam. With RSs facing, 3¼mm
needles and red, pick up and k 24 sts down left front
neck, 16 sts from centre front, 24 sts up right front
neck, 40 sts across back neck. Cast on 8 sts (112
sts). Now work in rib and stripes, setting colours as
follows: 8 sts each in blue, brown, yellow, green,
blue, brown, yellow, green, blue, brown, yellow,
green, blue, brown. Work in k1, p1 rib in colours as
set for 2 rows.
Next row: rib in correct colours to last 5 sts, cast off
2 sts, rib to end.
Next row: rib 3, cast on 2 sts, rib in correct colours
to end.
Now cont in rib and stripes for 5cm, working
buttonholes as described when neckband measures
2.5cm and 5cm. Work 2 rows after the last
buttonhole. Cast off ribwise in correct colours.

MAKING UP

Join left shoulder seam. Attach buttons to match the
buttonholes. Join the sleeves to the body using
narrow back stitch, and use flat seams for the side
and sleeve seams.

HIEROGLYPHICS SWEATER

THE MOTIFS on this crunchy cotton bouclé jumper have been adapted from Egyptian hieroglyphics. The one-size jumper, which will fit bust size 96cm (38in), is worked in stocking stitch throughout in a selection of bright colours that will complement a summer wardrobe.

Materials
Melinda Coss cotton bouclé mix – 450gm white; 100gm black; 50gm blue; 50gm green; 50gm pink, 5 buttons, 7mm in diameter.

Needles
One pair of 4mm needles; one pair of $3^3/_4$mm needles. Stitch holders.

Tension
Using 4mm needles and measured over st st, 20 sts and 29 rows = 10cm square.

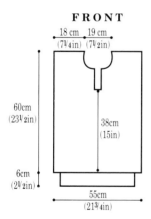

FRONT

18 cm (7¼in) 19 cm (7½in)

60cm (23½in)

38cm (15in)

6cm (2½in)

55cm (21¾in)

FRONT
With $3^3/_4$mm needles and black, cast on 110 sts.
Row 1: k2 black, p2 white, repeat to last 2 sts, k2 black.
Row 2: p2 black, k2 white, repeat to last 2 sts, p2 black. Repeat these 2 rows until rib measures 6cm, ending on a row 2.
Next row (RS): change to 4mm needles and begin to foll chart, working in st st for 110 rows. **Make neck opening.**
Next row (RS): k50, slip rem sts on to a spare needle and cont on this first set of sts only. Foll chart to neck shaping.
Next row (WS): cast off 4 sts at the beg of next row and 1 st at neck edge on the foll 4 rows. Then cast off 1 st at neck edge on the 6 foll alt rows (36 sts). Work straight for 6 rows, slip rem 36 sts on to a spare needle. Return to held sts, slip centre 10 sts on to a safety pin and foll chart to neck shaping. Shape as for other side of neck. When chart is complete, leave rem 36 sts on a spare needle.

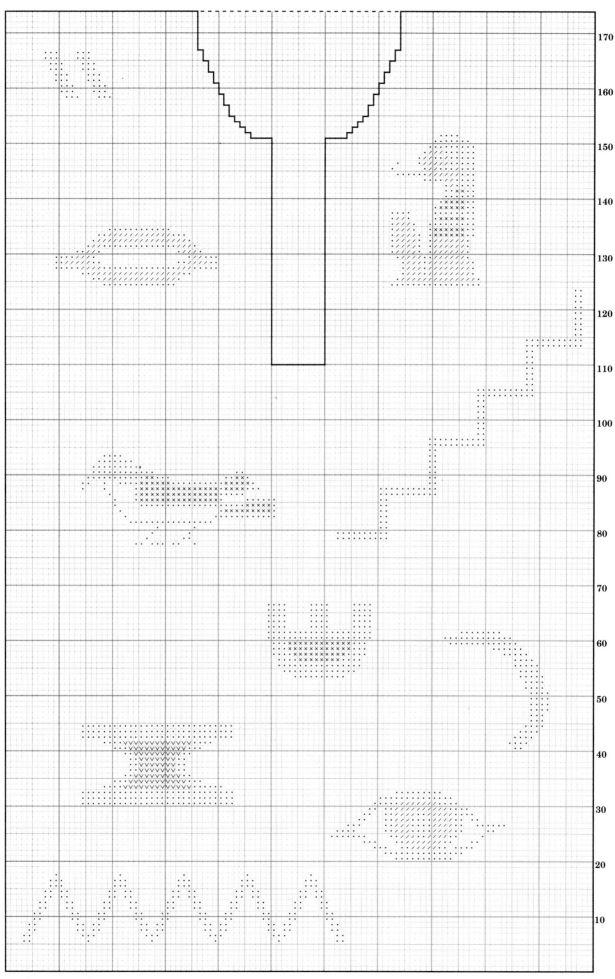

BACK AND FRONT   The dotted line indicates the back neck shaping

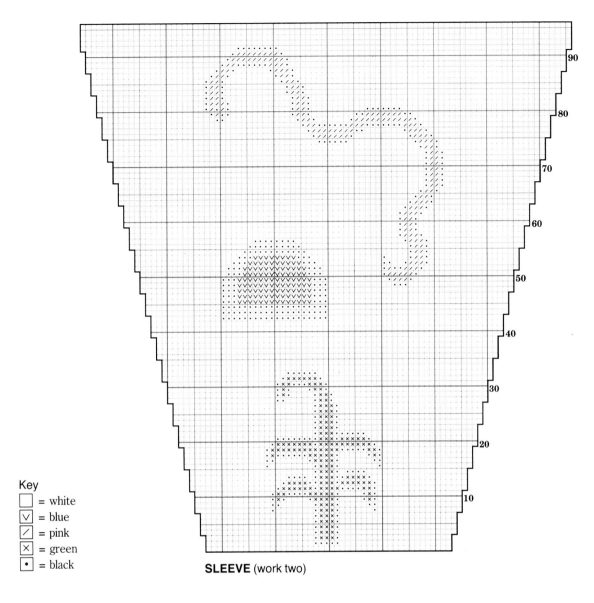

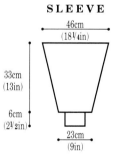

Key

- □ = white
- ☑ = blue
- ⊘ = pink
- ☒ = green
- ⊡ = black

SLEEVE (work two)

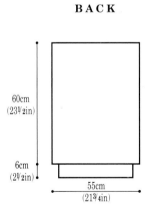

B A C K

60cm
(23½in)

6cm
(2½in)

55cm
(21¾in)

B A C K

Work as for front but ignore neck opening and shapings. When row 174 is complete, slip all sts on to a spare needle, placing markers after the 36th st and the foll 38th st for shoulders.

S L E E V E S

(Both alike) With 3¾mm needles and black, cast on 42 sts. Work in rib as for front for 6cm, inc 4 sts

S L E E V E

46cm
(18¼in)

33cm
(13in)

6cm
(2½in)

23cm
(9in)

evenly across the last row (46 sts). Change to 4mm needles and begin to foll sleeve chart in st st, inc 1 st each end of every fourth row until there are 92 sts. Work 4 rows without shaping. Cast off loosely.

Lay front over back, WSs facing each other. With black, k tog and cast off the first shoulder with the first 36 sts of the back, forming a black ridge on the RS of your work. Slip centre 38 sts on to a spare needle and cast off second shoulder as for first shoulder.

NECKBAND

With RS of work facing, 3³/₄mm needles, white yarn and starting at the left front opening, pick up 22 sts up left front, 38 sts held for back and 22 sts down right front (82 sts).

Row 1: k2 black, p2 white. Rep to last 2 sts, k2 black.

Row 2: p2 black, k2 white. Rep to last 2 sts, p2 black.

Repeat these 2 rows until work measures 2.5cm, ending with a row 2. Cast off in black.

BUTTONBAND

With 3³/₄mm needles and white, pick up the 10 sts held at neck. Work in st st in white until band fits neatly up side opening to the top of the neck rib when slightly stretched. Stitch neatly to left side. Place a pin 3 rows down from the top of the band and a second pin 3 rows up from the bottom to mark button positions. Space 3 pins evenly between them.

BUTTONHOLE BAND

With 3³/₄mm needles and white, pick up 10 st **over** those already picked up at base of neck opening. Working in st st stripes of 2 rows white, 2 rows black, make a buttonhole on the third row as follows: k4, cast off 2, k4. Keeping in stripe sequence, cast on 2 sts over those cast off on the next row. Repeat the buttonhole rows to correspond with pins on buttonband. When last buttonhole is complete, st st 2 rows, cast off. Stitch into position.

MAKING UP

Join the sleeves to the jumper, and use a flat seam to join the side and sleeve seams. Sew the buttons into position.

HUNGARIAN FOLK ART CARDIGAN

THIS SHORT CARDIGAN is decorated with popular Hungarian folk art motifs that reflect the flamboyant tastes and culture of villagers. Knitted in DK wool and angora, the two sizes quoted will fit bust sizes 86/96cm (34/38in). The cardigan should be worked in reverse stocking stitch, using the intarsia method.

Materials

Melinda Coss DK wool – 325/425gm black (A); Melinda Coss angora – less than 50gm each of green (B), white (C), fuchsia (D) and red (E).

Needles

One pair of 3¹/₄mm needles; one pair of 4mm needles; one short cable needle. 6 buttons, 1.5cm in diameter.

Tension

Using 4mm needles and measured over st st, 24 sts and 32 rows = 10cm square.

N.B. The cardigan is worked in reverse st st – i.e., purl is RS. The motifs and cables are worked in st st – i.e., knit is RS.

BACK

With 3¹/₄mm needles and A, cast on 116 sts. Work in rib as follows.
Row 1: k4D, *(p2A, k2A) twice, p2A*, k4E. Rep from * to *, k4C. Rep from * to *, k4B. Rep from * to *, k4D. Rep from * to *, k4B. Rep from * to *, k4C. Rep from * to *, k4E. Rep from * to *, k4D.
Row 2: p4D, *(k2A, p2A) twice, k2A*, p4E. Rep from * to *, p4C. Rep from * to *, p4B. Rep from * to *, p4D. Rep from * to *, p4B. Rep from * to *, p4C. Rep from * to *, p4E. Rep from * to *, p4D.
Repeat last 2 rows once more.
Next row: work as for row 1, but on each set of 4 coloured k sts make a cable as follows: using col as set, sl 2 sts on to a cable needle and hold at front of work, k2, k2 sts from cable needle. Work row 2. Repeat the last 6 rows 5 times more.

BACK

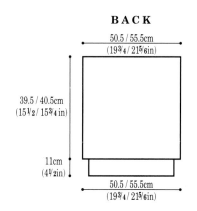

BACK

50.5 / 55.5cm
(19³/₄ / 21⁵/₆in)

39.5 / 40.5cm
(15¹/₂ / 15³/₄ in)

11cm
(4¹/₂in)

50.5 / 55.5cm
(19³/₄ / 21⁵/₆in)

The red lines indicate the area of the charts to be worked
to complete the smaller size

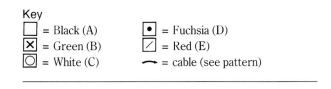

Key
☐ = Black (A)   • = Fuchsia (D)
☒ = Green (B)   ⁄ = Red (E)
◯ = White (C)   ⌒ = cable (see pattern)

Work rows 1 and 2 again, then work row 1 increasing
5/17 sts evenly across row (121/133 sts). Change to
4mm needles and A, and begin to foll chart, working
background in reverse st st (i.e., first row WS, k,
and work all motifs and cable bands in st st – i.e., k is
RS). When an arrow is indicated on chart, slip 2 sts
on to a cable needle and hold at front of work, k2, k2
from cable needle.
When the chart is completed, cast off 41/46 sts,
work to end of row. Cast off 41/46 sts at the beg of
the next row. Cast off remaining 39/41 sts.

LEFT FRONT

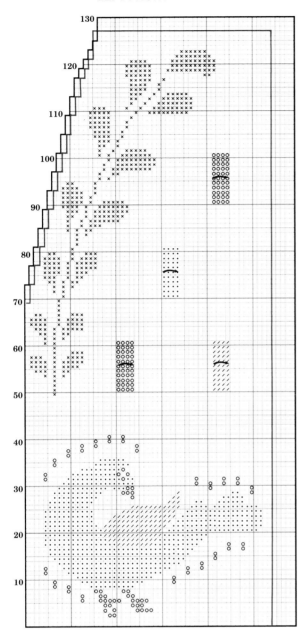

LEFT FRONT

With 3¹/₄mm needles and A, cast on 52/56 sts.
Row 1 second size only: k4E; both sizes: *(p2A, k2A) twice, p2A*, k4C. Rep from * to *, k4B. Rep from * to *, k4D. Rep from * to *.
Row 2: *(k2A, p2A) twice, k2A*, p4D. Rep from * to *, p4B. Rep from * to *, p4C. Rep from * to *; second size only: p4E.
Rep the last 2 rows once more, then work cable row as for back, work row 2, rep the last 6 rows 5 times more, then work rows 1 and 2 once more. Work row 1 and inc 2/3 sts across this row of rib (54/59 sts). Change to 4mm needles and A, and begin to foll chart, working background in reverse st st and all motifs in st st. Work straight to neck shaping. Dec 1 st at end of next row and 12/11 following fourth rows. Dec 1 st at same edge on next 2/4 alt rows. Work until chart is complete. Cast off rem 39/43 sts.

RIGHT FRONT

Work as for left front, reversing the shapings and image.

SLEEVES

(Both alike) With 3¹/₄mm needles and A, cast on 52 sts.
Row 1: *(p2A, k2A) twice, p2A*, k4B. Rep from * to *, k4C. Rep from * to *, k4D. Rep from * to *.
Row 2: *(k2A, p2A) twice, k2A*, p4D. Rep from * to *, p4C. Rep from * to *, p4B. Rep from * to *.
Repeat the last 2 rows once more, then rep row 1, working cables as for back on sets of 4 k sts. Work row 2. Rep the last 6 rows 4 times more, then work rows 1 and 2. Repeat row 1, inc 5/9 sts evenly across this row (57/61 sts). Change to 4mm needles and A, and begin to foll chart, working background in reverse st st and motifs in st st, first row WS, k. **At the same time first size:** inc 1 st each end of the fifth row and the 16 following sixth rows (91 sts), then inc 1 st each end of the next 2 eighth rows (95 sts). Work straight until chart is complete, cast off loosely. **Second size:** inc 1 st each end of the fourth row and the 4 foll fourth rows (81 sts). Then inc 1 st each end of every sixth row until you have 103 sts. Work straight until chart is complete, cast off loosely.

BUTTONBAND

With 3¹/₄mm needles and E, cast on 10 sts.
Row 1: k1, p2, k4, p2, k1.
Row 2: k3, p4, k3.
Repeat the last 2 rows once more.
Next row: k1, p2, sl next 2 sts on to a cable needle and hold at front of work, k2, k2 from cable needle,

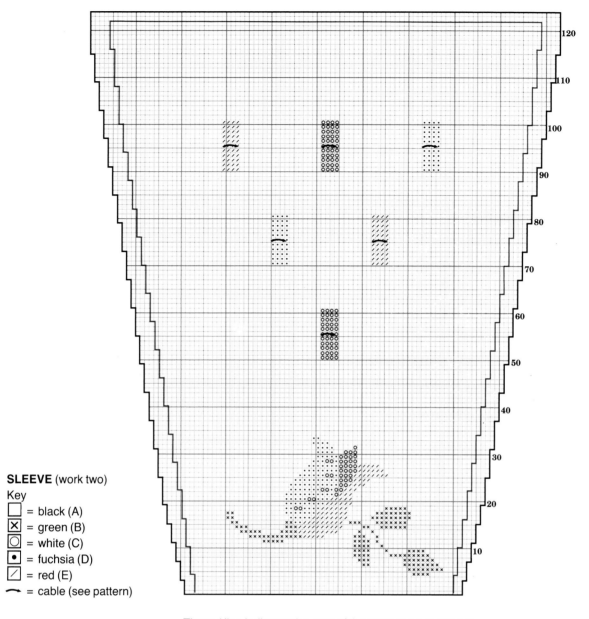

SLEEVE (work two)

Key

☐ = black (A)
☒ = green (B)
○ = white (C)
● = fuchsia (D)
⟋ = red (E)
⌣ = cable (see pattern)

The red line indicates the area of the chart to be worked to complete the smaller size

p2, k1. Work row 2. Cont by repeating these 6 rows until band fits neatly up left front, to centre back neck. With pins, mark positions for 6 buttons between cables with the bottom button 6 rows from lower edge, and the top button just below the beginning of neck shaping.

BUTTONHOLE BAND

Work as for buttonband but use B and make buttonholes on RS rows to correspond with pins as foll: k1, p2, sl1, k2tog, psso, k1, p2, k1.
On return row, p1, k2, p1, cast on 2 sts, k2, p1.
Continue band as set until it fits neatly to centre back neck. Cast off.

MAKING UP

Join shoulder seams. Join the sleeves to the body, join side and sleeve seams. Use a flat seam to attach the front bands into position. Sew on buttons to match.

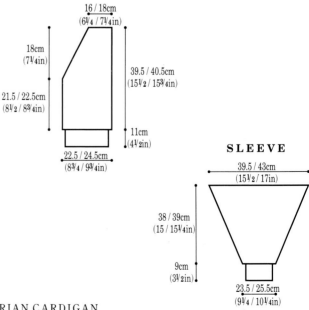

LEFT FRONT

16 / 18cm
(6¼ / 7¼in)

18cm
(7¼in)

39.5 / 40.5cm
(15½ / 15¾in)

21.5 / 22.5cm
(8½ / 8¾in)

11cm
(4½in)

22.5 / 24.5cm
(8¾ / 9¾in)

SLEEVE

39.5 / 43cm
(15½ / 17in)

38 / 39cm
(15 / 15¼in)

9cm
(3½in)

23.5 / 25.5cm
(9¼ / 10¼in)

INDIAN SUMMER JACKET AND LEGGINGS

THIS SILKY, TAILORED JACKET with leggings is based on a West Indian theatre costume devised by the Russian designer Erté. The garments, quoted in bust sizes 86/92cm (34/36in) or UK dress sizes 10/12, are worked in mercerized cotton.

Materials

Jacket: Melinda Coss 6-ply mercerized cotton – 500/550gm crimson (A); 150gm purple (B); 100gm gold (C); 25gm lilac (D). 31 drop pearl beads, 31 pearls, 17 buttons, 1.5cm in diameter.
Leggings: Melinda Coss 6-ply mercerized cotton – 400/500gm purple (B); 100gm gold. 90cm elastic, 2cm wide.

Needles

One pair of $3^1/4$mm needles; one pair of $3^3/4$mm needles; one pair of 4mm needles. Stitch holders.

Tension

Jacket: using $3^3/4$mm needles and measured over st st, 24 sts and 29 rows = 10cm square. Leggings: using 4mm needles and measured over st st, 24 sts and 29 rows = 10cm square.

JACKET BACK

With $3^3/4$mm needles and A, cast on 112/134 sts and work in st st for 7 rows. K 1 row (to form a hemline). Working in st st and starting with a k row, begin to foll chart until row 72 is complete.
Row 73: k38/49 sts from chart, sl1, k1, psso, k32, k2tog, work chart to end.
Row 74 and all alt rows: keep chart correct.
Row 75: work chart for 37/48 sts, sl1, k1, psso, k32, k2tog, work chart to end.
Row 77: work chart for 36/47 sts, sl1, k1, psso, k32, k2tog, work chart to end.
Row 79: k35/46 sts from chart, sl1, k1, psso, work chart for 32 sts, k2tog, work chart to end.
Row 81: k34/45 sts from chart, sl1, k1, psso, work chart for 32 sts, k2tog, work chart to end.
Cont dec on every alt row as set until row 102 is complete.
Row 103: k23/34 sts from chart, sl1, k1, psso, work chart for 32 sts, k2tog, work chart to end.
Row 105: k23/34 sts from chart, m1, work chart for 34 sts, m1, work chart to end.
Row 107: k23/34 sts from chart, m1, work chart for 36 sts, m1, work chart to end.
Row 109: k23/34 sts from chart, m1, work chart for 38 sts, m1, work chart to end.

The red line indicates the area of
the chart to be worked to
complete the smaller size

Key
A = crimson
B = purple
C = gold
D = lilac

BACK

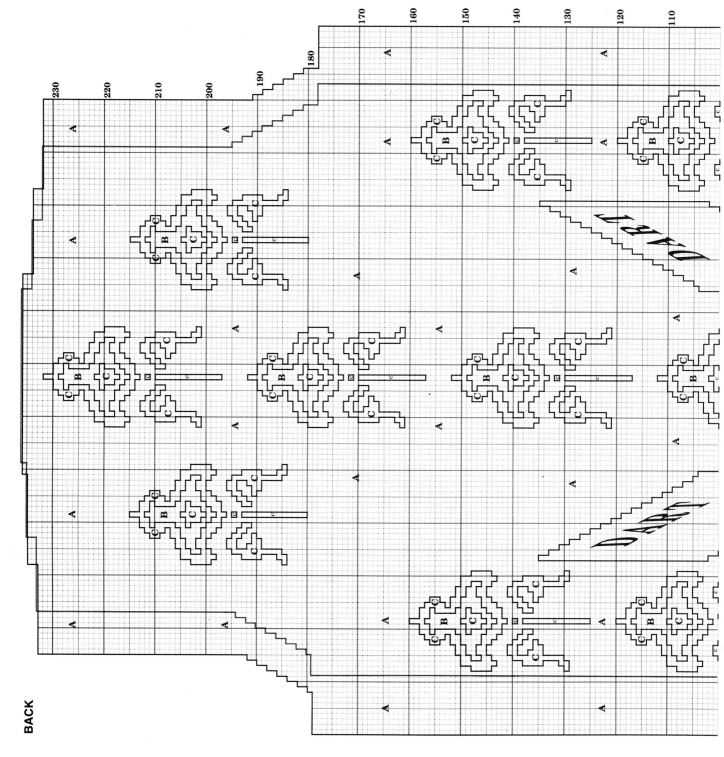

Cont inc on every alt row as set until row 133 is complete.

Row 134: work from chart.

Row 135: k23/34 sts from chart, m1, work chart for 64 sts, m1, work chart to end.

Row 136: work from chart.

The dart shapings are now complete. Cont to foll chart until row 178 has been worked. **Shape armholes.**

Row 179: keeping chart correct, cast off 4/8 sts at the beg of this row and row 180.

Row 181: work chart to last 2 sts, k2tog.

Row 182: work chart to last 2 sts, p2tog.

Cont as set, dec 1 st at the end of every row until 88/105 sts remain. Cont to foll chart until row 232 has been completed.

Row 233: in A, cast off 14/17 sts, k to end.

Row 234: in A, cast off 14/17 sts, p to end.

Rep the last 2 rows once more, leave rem sts on a holder for the neckband.

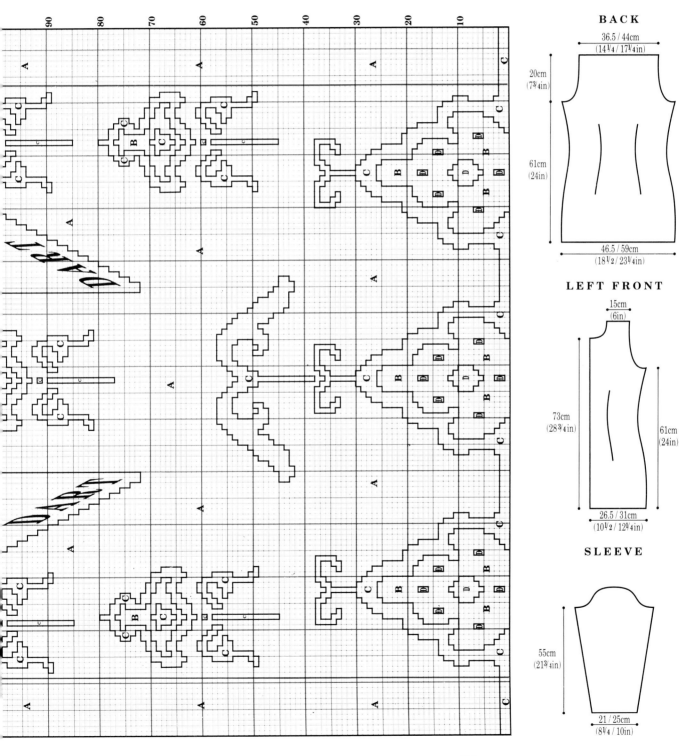

Row 74: follow chart.
Row 75: k37/48 sts from chart, sl1, k1, psso, work chart to end.
Cont dec every alt row until row 102 is complete.
Row 103: k23/34 sts from chart, sl1, k1, psso, work chart to end.
Row 105 (and all foll alt rows to row 135): k23/34 sts from chart, m1, work chart to end.
Work straight from chart until row 178 is complete.
Shape armhole.
Row 179: cast off 4/8 sts and work chart to end. Dec 1 st at armhole edge on every foll alt row until row 195/191 has been worked, then cont straight from chart until row 212/212 has been worked.
Row 213: work chart to last 12 sts and leave these on a holder for neck edge.
Row 214: p from chart.
Now, keeping chart correct, dec 1 st at front neck edge on every row until 27/36 sts remain. Work chart without further shaping to shoulder. **Shape shoulder:** cast off 14/17 sts, k to end. Work 1 row and cast off rem sts.

RIGHT FRONT

Work as for left front, reversing all shapings. Work dart shaping decrease as k2tog instead of sl1, k1, psso.

SLEEVES

(Both alike) With 3³/₄mm needles and B, cast on 50/60 sts and work in st st for 7 rows. K 1 row to

LEFT FRONT

With 3³/₄mm needles and A, cast on 64/75 sts and work in st st for 7 rows. K 1 row to form a hemline. Starting with a k row, work in st st from the chart for the left front, working rows 1–72 inclusive.
Row 73: k38/49 sts from chart, sl1 k1, psso, work chart to end.

LEFT FRONT
The red line indicates the area of the chart to be worked to complete the smaller size

Key
A = crimson
B = purple
C = gold
D = lilac

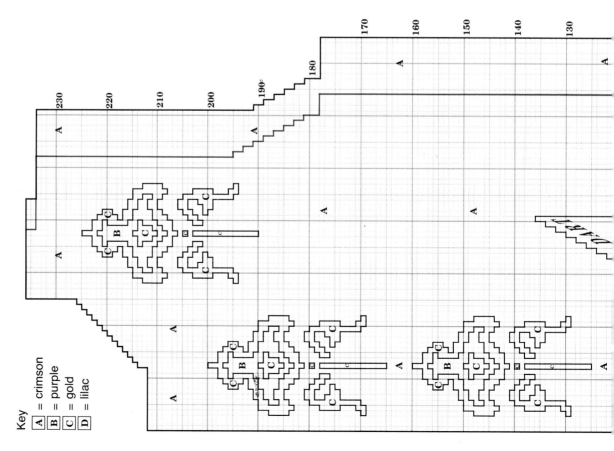

form a hemline. Now work from chart, inc 1 st at each end of every sixth row. **At the same time**, when 65 rows have been completed, work as follows.

Row 66: change to A, inc into first st, *p2, k2, rep from * to last 3 sts, k2, p1, inc in last st. Keeping rib correct, work a further 5 rows. Now cont from chart in st st, inc as set until row 137/140 has been completed. **Shape top:** cast off 4/8 sts at the beg of the next 2 rows. Now, keeping chart correct, dec 1 st at each end of every row until 52/55 sts remain. Cast off all sts.

BUTTONHOLE BAND

With 3³/₄mm needles and A, cast on 8 sts and work in st st for 2 rows. **Buttonhole row 1 (RS): k3, cast off 2 sts, k3. Buttonhole row 2: p3, cast on 2 sts, p3, work 9 rows in st st. Buttonhole Row 3: as row 2. Buttonhole row 4: as row 1. Work 9 rows in st st**. Repeat from ** to ** 7 times, then work the first two buttonhole rows again. Work 3 rows in st st. Cast off.

BUTTONBAND

With 3³/₄mm needles and A, cast on 8 sts and work in garter st until band reaches neck shaping when slightly stretched.

COLLAR

Join shoulder seams. With RS facing, 3³/₄mm needles and A, pick up and k approx 24/28 sts up right side neck, 32/37 sts across back neck, approx 24/28 sts down left side neck. Working in p, inc 8 sts evenly around next row, then work in st st for 9 rows. Next row (WS): k 1 row to form a ridge, then, starting with a k row, work in st st for 10 rows. Cast off loosely using a larger needle.

MAKING UP

Set the sleeves into place, easing any fullness to the top, and sew into armholes, using narrow back stitch. Pin the buttonhole band into place on right front (to fit as a concealed fly buttonband) as follows. With WSs together, pin band so that the cast-on edge fits along the hem ridge row (on inside). Sew into place along ridge row, up inside edge of front and along 8 cast-off sts at front neck shaping. Sew the side seams, turn the hem to inside and catch into place along inside edge. Sew the buttonband neatly to the left front edge (pinning into place first). Join the sleeve seams in correct colours. Sew on buttons to match buttonholes. Turn collar to inside at ridge row and catch into place. Sew pearls into position on motifs, using the photograph as a guide.

LEGS

(Make 2) Using 3³/₄mm needles and B, cast on 58/80 sts. Work in k1, p1 rib for 16 rows. Change to 4mm needles and begin leg chart, working in st st for 17 rows. Inc 1 st each end of next row and every foll sixth row until you have completed 193 rows, excluding the rib (118/140 sts).

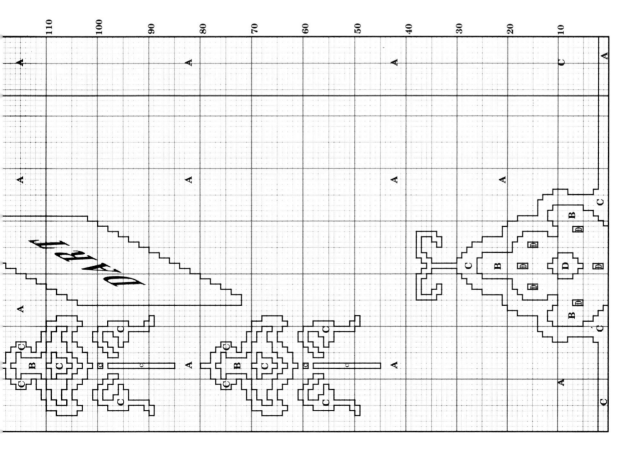

CROTCH

Cast off 10/14 sts at the beg of the next 2 rows (98/112 sts). Work straight until chart is complete, then, **for larger size only**, work an extra 20 rows in base colour. **Both sizes:** change to $3^{1}/_{4}$mm needles and work in k1, p1 rib for 16 rows. Cast off loosely.

MAKING UP

Using a flat seam, join the leg and rise seams. Turn the waist band hem inwards and slip stitch into position, leaving a gap for the elastic to be inserted. Using a safety pin, thread the elastic through to fit, overlap the ends and sew securely together.

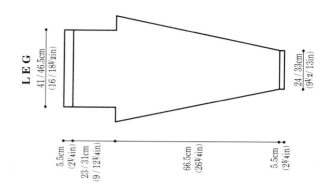

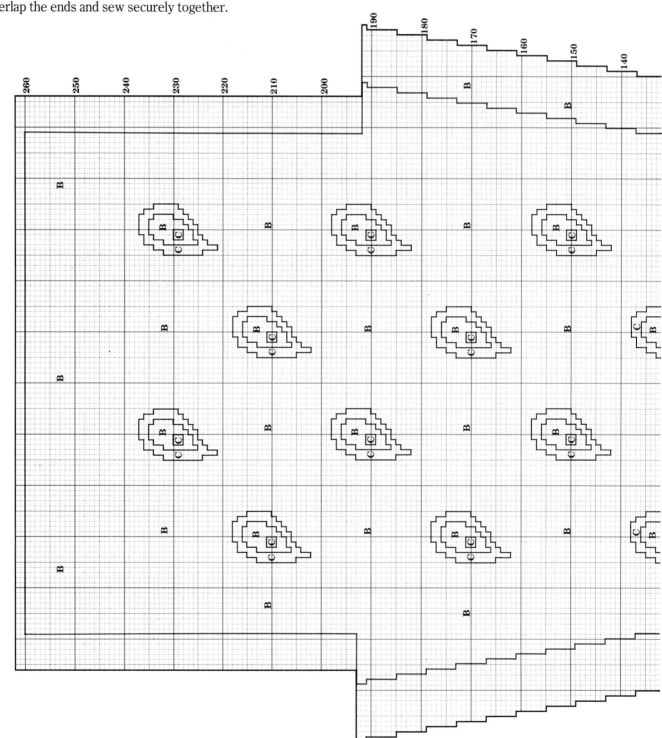

LEGGINGS

The red line indicates the area of
the chart to be worked to
complete the smaller size

Key
B = purple
C = gold

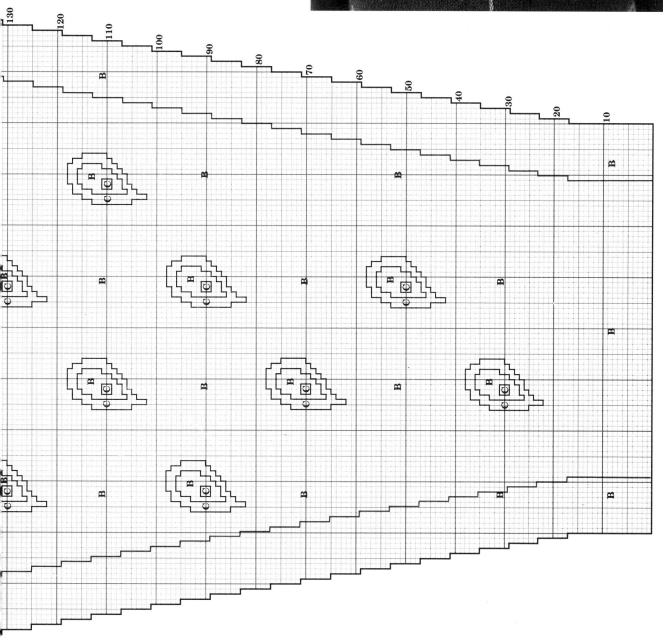

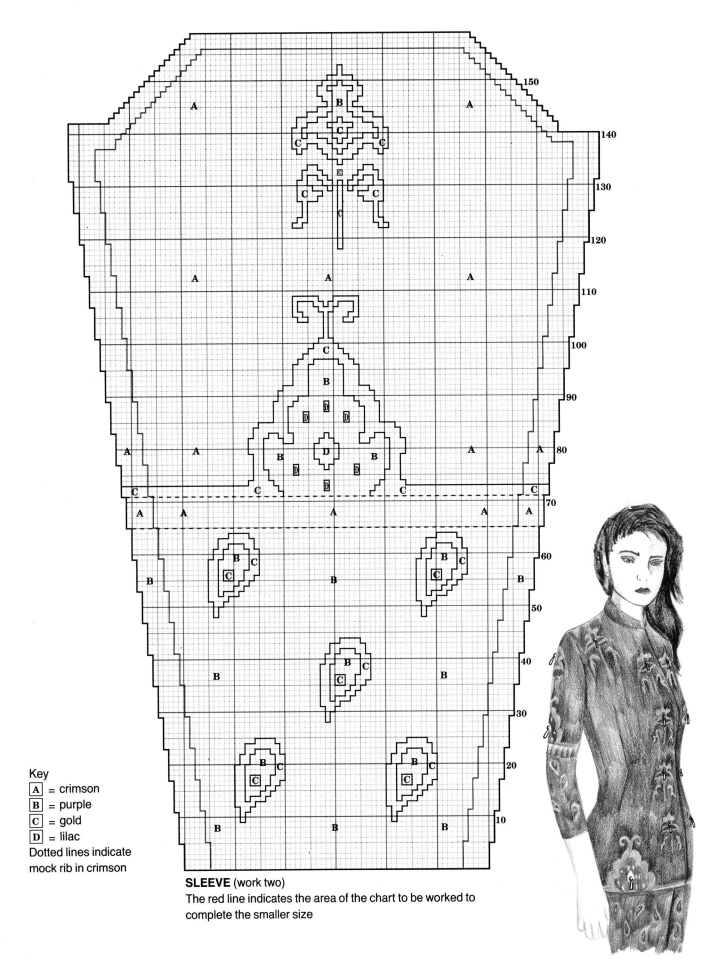

Key

A = crimson
B = purple
C = gold
D = lilac

Dotted lines indicate
mock rib in crimson

SLEEVE (work two)
The red line indicates the area of the chart to be worked to
complete the smaller size

INDONESIAN TEXTILE SWEATER

THE STYLIZED Indonesian horses on this sweater were taken from a woman's festive skirt, of the kind woven, using the Ikat method, on Sumba, one of the most southerly islands of the Malay archipelago. The sweater, which is worked in DK wool, will fit 106cm (42in) chest.

Materials

Melinda Coss DK wool – 700gm navy blue (lime); 125gm burgundy; 100gm ecru; 100gm petrol blue.

Needles

One pair of 4mm needles; one pair of $3^{1}/_{4}$mm needles. Stitch holders.

Tension

Using 4mm needles and measured over st st, 24 sts and 32 rows = 10cm square.

N.B. When working Fair Isle stripes, strand and weave yarn loosely across no more than 5 sts in order to keep the fabric elastic.

BACK, FRONT AND SLEEVES The red lines indicate the front neck shaping and the area of the chart to be worked to complete both sleeves

Key

▢ = navy blue

⌒ = k on WS and p on RS of work in navy blue

↓ = c8F

↘ = c4F

A = burgundy

B = petrol blue

C = cream

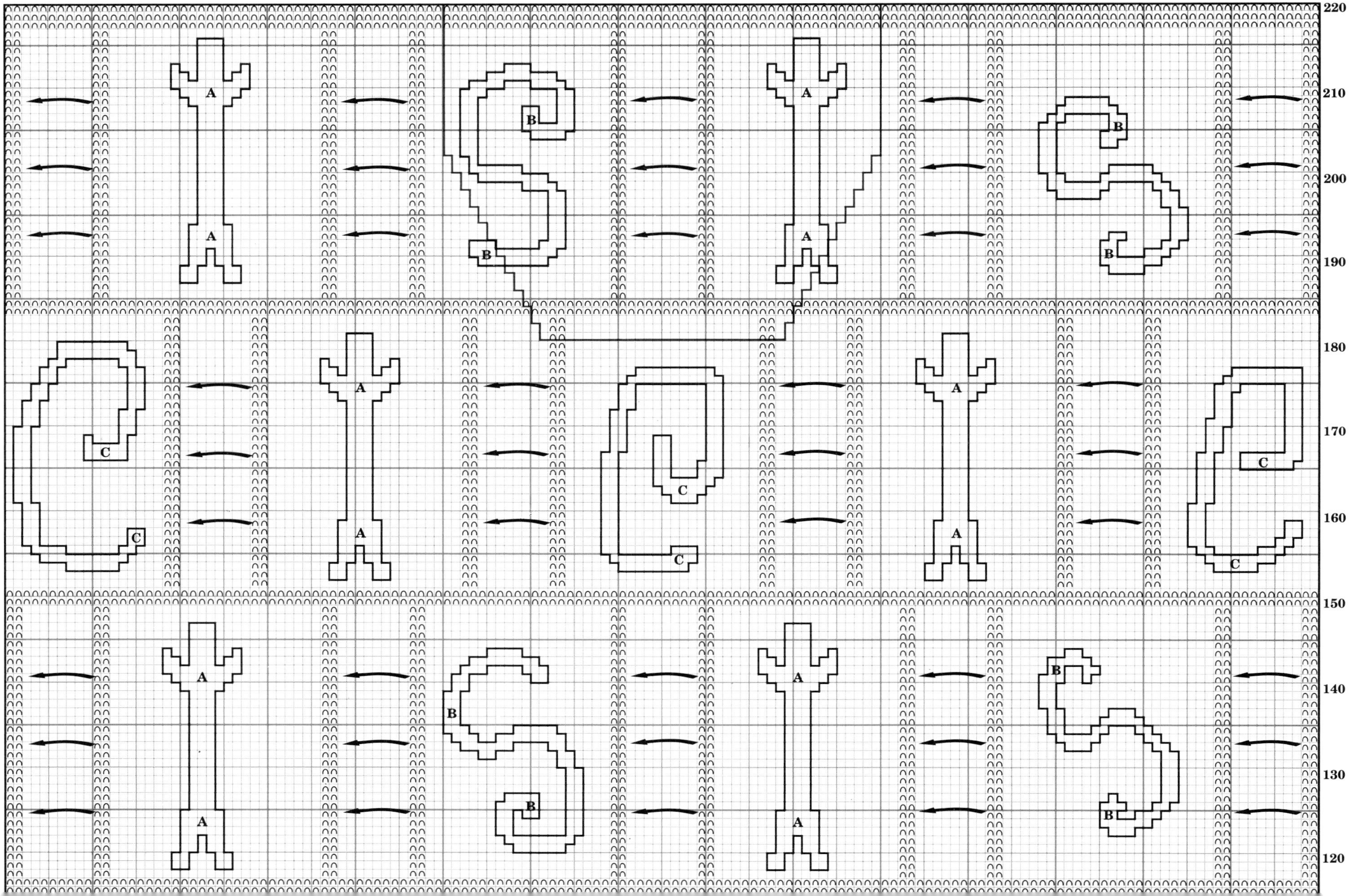

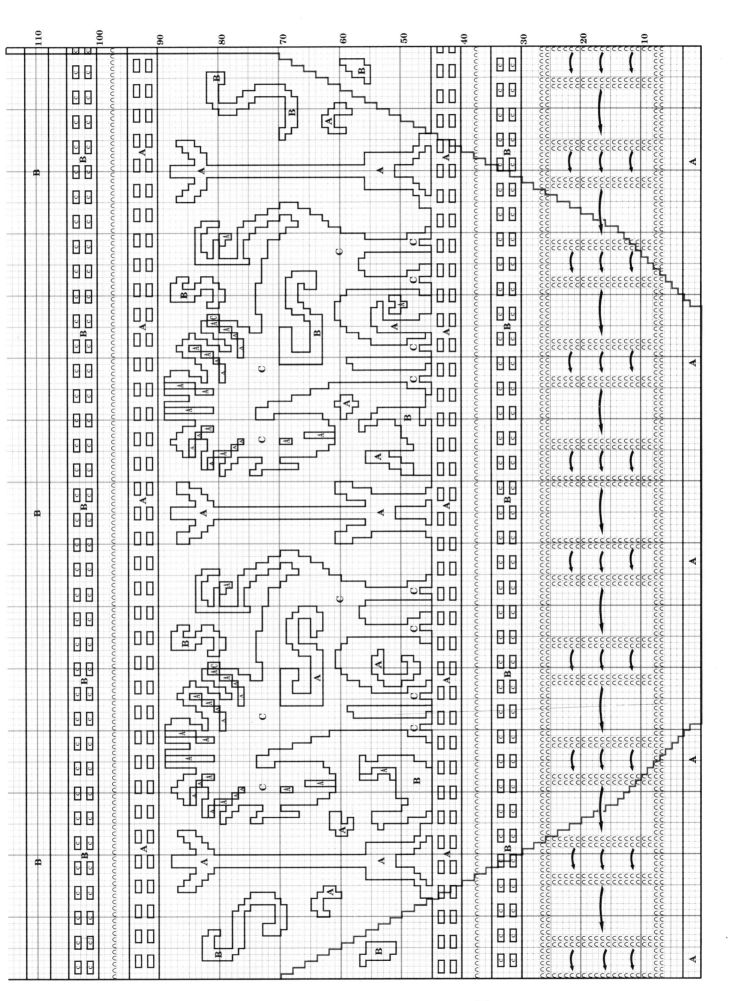

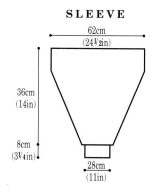

FRONT

Using 3¹/₄mm needles and navy blue, cast on 140 sts and work in k2, p2 rib for 9cm. Inc 10 sts evenly across last row of rib (150 sts). Change to 4mm needles * and begin to foll chart for front in st st, working cables as indicated, to neck shaping. **Shape neck.**

Next row (RS): work patt for 89 sts, sl the last 28 sts just worked on to a st holder, patt to end. Cont on this last set of 61 sts only as follows. Dec 1 st at neck edge on every alt row until 50 sts remain. Cont without further shaping until chart is complete. Leave sts on a holder. With WS facing, rejoin yarn to the remaining sts at neck edge and shape as for the other side.

are 93 sts. Cont by inc each end of every alt row until there are 149 sts. Cont without further shaping until sleeve chart is complete. Cast off loosely.

With RSs of work facing each other and using navy blue wool, k right shoulder seam together.

NECKBAND

With RS facing, 3¹/₄mm needles and navy blue, pick up and k 30 sts down left front neck, 28 sts from front neck st holder, 30 sts up right front neck and 50 sts across back neck (138 sts). Work in k2, p2 rib for 9cm. Cast off loosely in rib.

MAKING UP

Knit left shoulder seam together. Fold neckband inwards and slip st cast-off edge to pick-up edge. Join the sleeves to the body using narrow back stitch, and join the side and sleeve seams with flat seams.

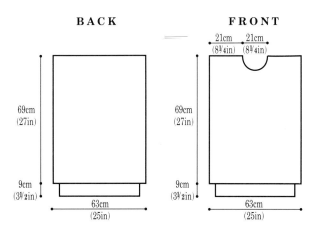

BACK

Work as for front to *. Cont in st st until chart is complete, working cables where indicated. Leave rem 150 sts on a spare needle.

SLEEVES

(Both alike) Using 3¹/₄mm needles and navy blue, cast on 52 sts and work in k2, p2 rib for 8cm, inc 15 sts evenly across last row of rib (67 sts). Change to 4mm needles and begin to work area outlined in red on the chart. **At the same time** inc 1 st at each end of the third row and then every foll row until there

JAPANESE PRINT COAT

THIS MOHAIR COAT is based on a famous print by Toshusai Sharaku. The coat, which is worked in stocking stitch, will fit up to bust size 96–102cm (38–40in), and the cocoon shape is flattering to all sizes.

Materials

Melinda Coss mohair – 350gm green; 250gm rose; 75gm white; 75gm black; 50gm yellow; 25gm khaki; 25gm coffee; 25gm ginger; 25gm silver grey. Grey 4-ply wool for embroidery.

Needles

One pair of $5^{1}/_{2}$mm needles.

Tension

Using $5^{1}/_{2}$mm needles and measured over st st, 16 sts and 16 rows = 10cm square.

BACK

Using $5^{1}/_{2}$mm needles and green, cast on 112 sts. Begin to foll chart for back in st st to raglan shaping. Cast off 2 sts at the beg of the next 2 rows, then dec 1 st each end of every alt row until chart is complete. Cast off rem 18 sts.

LEFT FRONT

Using $5^{1}/_{2}$mm needles and green, cast on 8 sts. Begin to foll chart in st st, casting on 7 sts at the end of the third row and 5 sts at the end of the 2 foll alt rows. Cast on 3 sts at the end of the next alt row and 2 sts at the end of the foll alt row. Then inc 1 st at the end of the next alt row and 1 st at the end of the foll 18 rows (49 sts). Work 1 row, then inc 1 st at the end of the next row and the 9 foll alt rows (59 sts).

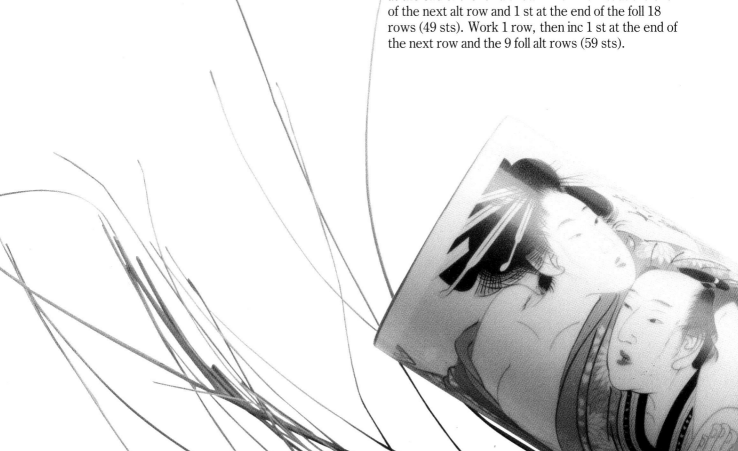

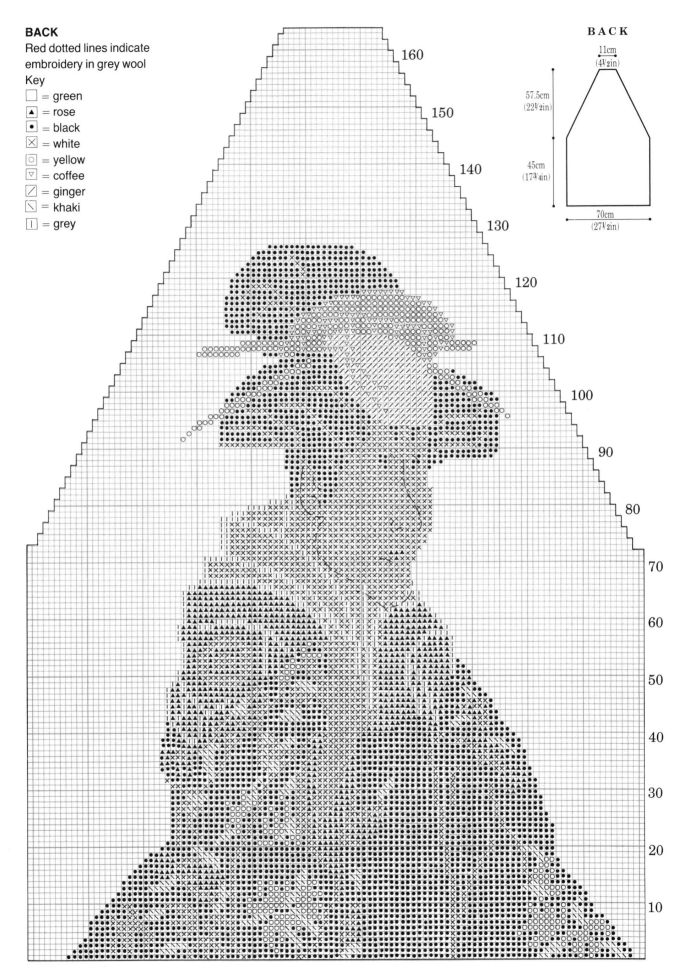

BACK

Red dotted lines indicate embroidery in grey wool

Key

☐ = green

▲ = rose

● = black

☒ = white

⊙ = yellow

▽ = coffee

╱ = ginger

╲ = khaki

▯ = grey

BACK

11cm
(4½in)

57.5cm
(22½in)

45cm
(17¾in)

70cm
(27½in)

160

150

140

130

120

110

100

90

80

70

60

50

40

30

20

10

LEFT/FRONT

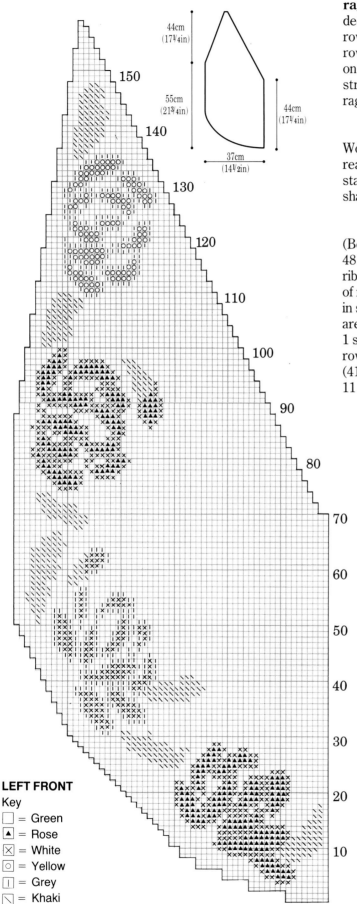

44cm
(17¼in)

55cm
(21¾in)

44cm
(17¼in)

37cm
(14½in)

150

140

130

120

110

100

90

80

70

60

50

40

30

20

10

LEFT FRONT

Key

☐ = Green

▲ = Rose

☒ = White

⊙ = Yellow

| = Grey

◺ = Khaki

Cont straight without further shaping until 70 rows have been worked from the beg of chart. **Shape raglan:** cast off 2 sts at the beg of the next row and dec 1 st at same edge on the foll 8 alt rows. Work 1 row. Cont to dec 1 st at armhole edge on every alt row and **shape neck** by casting off 1 st at neck edge on next row and the 11 foll sixth rows. Then work straight at neck edge, while continuing to shape raglan edge until 1 st rem. Fasten off.

RIGHT FRONT

Work as for left front but read chart in reverse – i.e., read chart from right to left in p, and left to right in k, starting with a p row, thus reversing chart and shapings.

SLEEVES

(Both alike) With 5½mm needles and rose, cast on 48 sts. Work 4 rows in garter st, then work in k6, p6 rib for 22 rows, inc 5 sts evenly across the last row of rib (53 sts). Change to khaki and begin to foll chart in st st, inc 1 st at each end of every row until there are 109 sts. Work 2 rows without shaping, then dec 1 st at each end of the next row and the 6 foll fourth rows. Dec 1 st at each end of every alt row 27 times (41 sts) then at each end of every row until you have 11 sts. Cast off.

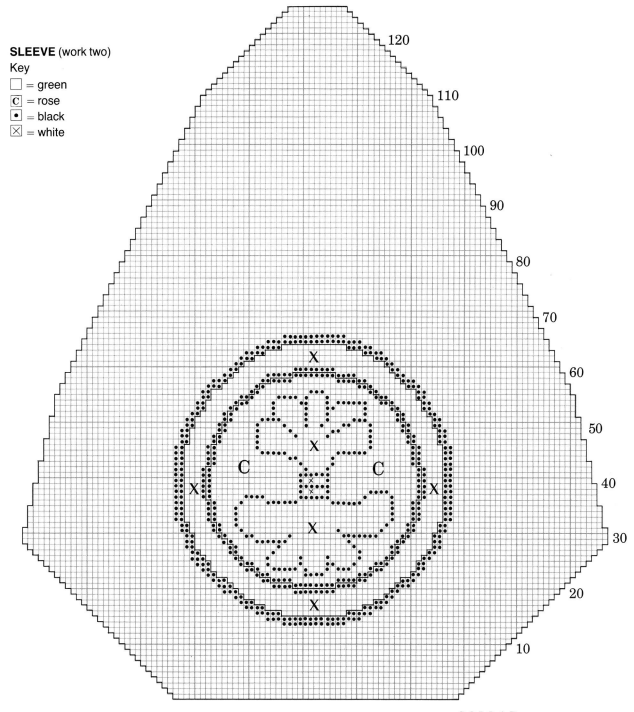

SLEEVE (work two)

Key

☐ = green

Ⓒ = rose

▪ = black

☒ = white

120
110
100
90
80
70
60
50
40
30
20
10

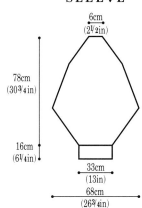

SLEEVE

6cm
(2¹/₂in)

78cm
(30³/₄in)

16cm
(6¹/₄in)

33cm
(13in)

68cm
(26³/₄in)

COLLAR

(Knitted in one piece) Using 5¹/₂mm needles and rose, cast on 30 sts.

Row 1: k6, * p6, k6, rep from *.

Row 2: p6, * k6, p6, rep from *.

Rep these 2 rows until the border fits all around the outer edge of the coat, beg and ending at centre back neck. Cast off.

MAKING UP

Join the raglan seams of back and sleeves, then join each front raglan to sleeves. Join the side and sleeve seams, using invisible seams throughout. Join border to coat, taking care not to pucker front curves. Use back stitch to embroider facial features in grey wool, as indicated on the chart.

KABUKI SWEATER

THIS DESIGN IS TAKEN from a series of Japanese costume prints. It is worked in DK wool and will fit up to chest size 96–102cm (38–40in). You should use the Fair Isle method on all repeating patterns and the intarsia method where large blocks of colours are indicated.

Materials

Melinda Coss DK wool – 300gm cream (A); 125gm coral (B); 100gm jade (C); 250gm black (D); 125gm tan (E).

Needles

One pair of 3¼mm needles, one pair 4mm needles.

Tension

Using 4mm needles and measured over Fair Isle pattern, 25 sts and 26 rows = 10cm square.

FRONT

With 3¼mm and D, cast on 141 sts.
Row 1: k1tbl, p1, rep to last st, k1tbl.
Row 2: p1, k1tbl, rep to last st, pl.
Rep these 2 rows until work measures 6.5cm, finishing on a row 2.
Change to 4mm needles and begin to foll chart, working in st st, using separate balls of yarn when it is carried over more than 10 sts. Take care not to pull areas of colour worked by the Fair Isle method too tightly, as an even tension is required throughout.* Work straight to **neck shaping.**
Next row: work patt for 70 sts and leave rem sts on a spare needle. Work on this first set of sts only, dec 1 st at neck edge on the next and every foll alt row until there are 63 sts. Then dec 1 st at same edge on every foll fourth row until 49 sts rem. Cont without further shaping until chart is complete. Cast off. With WS facing, rejoin yarn to rem sts. Cast off 1 st and work patt to end. Shape to match first side, work until chart is complete and cast off rem 49 sts.

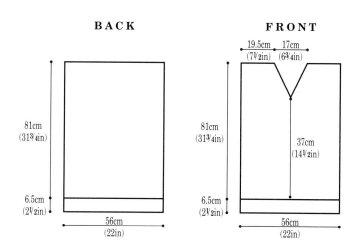

BACK

Work as for front to *. Begin to foll chart, but working from right to left in p and from left to right in k so that the image is reversed. Work until chart is complete. Cast off all sts.

LEFT SLEEVE

With 3¼mm needles and D, cast on 57 sts. Work in rib as for front until work measures 6.5cm, finishing on a row 2. Change to 4mm needles and begin to work checkered pattern, setting sts as follows.
Row 1: k1A, *k5C, k5A, k5C. Rep from * to last st, k1A.
Row 2: p1A, *p5C, p5A, p5C. Rep from * to last st, k1A.
Row 3: as row 1.

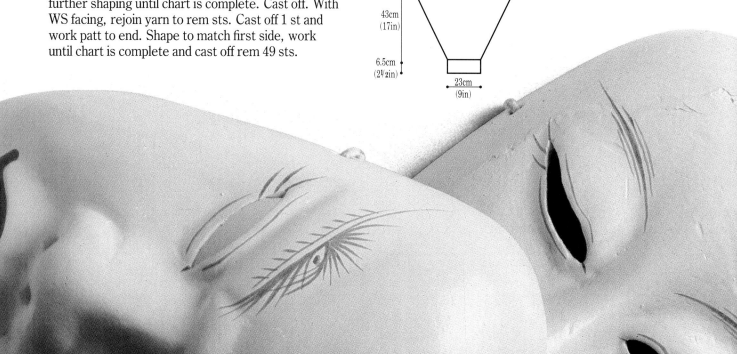

BACK, FRONT AND RIGHT SLEEVE

The dotted line indicates the back neck shaping; the red lines indicate the front neck shaping and the area to be worked to complete the right sleeve

Key

A = Cream   C = Jade
B = Coral   D = Black
             E = Tan

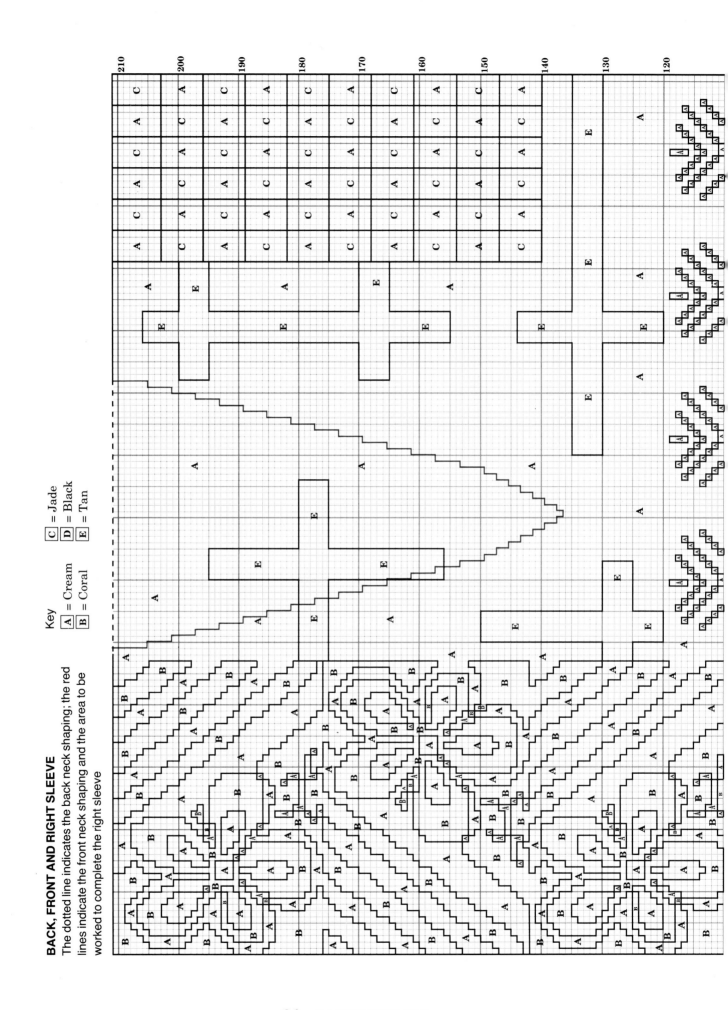

RIGHT SLEEVE

With 3¹/₄mm needles and D, cast on 57 sts. Work in rib as for front until work measures 6.5cm, finishing on a row 2. Change to 4mm needles and begin to work the checkered sleeve pattern on the chart, working in st st. Inc 1 st each end of every fourth row until there are 83 sts, then inc 1 st at each end of every sixth row until sleeve measures approximately 49.5cm (matching the left sleeve in length). Cast off. At the same time, when 40 rows of the chart are complete, rep from the beg, working increases in patt as set.
Join shoulder seams.

COLLAR

With 3¹/₄mm needles and D, cast on 29 sts. Working in twisted rib as for front, cast on 4 sts at the end of every row 12 times (77 sts). Cast on 87 sts at the end of the next 2 rows (251 sts). Cont in rib until side edge of collar measures 8cm, finishing on a row 2. Cast off loosely in rib.

MAKING UP

Join the sleeves to the jumper, then join side and sleeve seams. Pin cast-on edge of collar to neck, placing RS over left, and join to jumper using a flat seam. Slip stitch the short ends of the collar to the bottom edge of the V, as illustrated on the photograph.

Row 4: inc 1A, p1A, *p5C, p5A, p5C. Rep from * to last st, p1A, inc 1A.
Row 5: k2A, *k5C, k5A, k5C. Rep from * to last 2 sts, k2A.
Row 6: p2A, *p5C, p5A, p5C. Rep from * to last 2 sts, p2A.
Row 7: as row 5.
Row 8: inc 1C, p2C, *p5A, p5C, p5A. Rep from * to last 2 sts, p2C, inc 1C in last st.
Row 9: k3C, *k5A, k5C, k5A. Rep from * to last 3 sts, k3C.
Row 10: p3C, *p5A, p5C, p5A. Rep from * to last 3 sts, p3C.
Row 11: as row 9.
Row 12: inc 1C, p3C, *p5A, p5C, p5A. Rep from * to last 3 sts, p3C, inc 1C.
Row 13: k4C, *k5A, k5C, k5A. Rep from * to last 3 sts, k4C.
Row 14: p4C, *p5A, p5C, p5A. Rep from * to last 3 sts, p4C.
These 14 rows make up the pattern – i.e., blocks of 5 sts and 7 rows for each colour. Cont working in this sequence. **At the same time** cont to inc 1 st each end of every fourth row until you have 83 sts, then inc 1 st at each end of every sixth row until sleeve measures approximately 49.5cm, ending at the finish of a 7-row block of colour. Cast off.

KELIM JUMPER

THE MOTIFS on this richly coloured, Aran-weight jumper are typical of those used in carpet designs produced throughout the Middle East. The sweater, which will fit 96/112cm (38/44in) chest sizes, uses chenille yarn with the wool to emphasize the contrasting textures.

Materials

Melinda Coss Aran wool – 400/425gm garnet; 250gm peat; 250gm ecru; Melinda Coss chunky chenille – 75gm mid-blue; 75gm mushroom; 50gm pale green.

Needles

One pair of 4½mm needles, one pair of 3¾mm needles; 4 small cable needles; one short 3¼mm circular needle. Stitch holders.

Tension

Using 4½mm needles and measured over st st, 18 sts and 23 rows = 10cm square.

FRONT

With 3¾mm needles and peat, cast on 90/108 sts and work in single rib for 25 rows, inc 26/24 sts evenly across last row of rib (116/132 sts). Change to 4½mm needles and begin to foll chart, working in st st for 36 rows.
Next row (RS): work chart for 7/15 sts, slip next 2 sts on to a cable needle and hold at back of work, k2, then k2 from cable needle. Work chart for 15 sts.

Slip next 2 sts on to a cable needle and hold at front of work, k2, then k2 from cable needle. Work chart for 22 sts. Slip next 2 sts on to a cable needle and hold at back of work, k2, then k2 from cable needle. Work chart for 4 sts. Slip next 2 sts on to a cable needle and hold at front of work, k2, then k2 from cable needle. Work chart for 22 sts. Slip next 2 sts on to a cable needle and hold at back of work, k2, then k2 from cable needle. Work chart for 15 sts. Slip next 2 sts on to a cable needle and hold at front of work, k2, then k2 from cable needle. Work to end. This sets the cable pattern. Cable rows should be worked in peat throughout on every eighth row as set (see chart).
Cont following chart until row 94/97 has been worked. **Shape armholes:** cast off 5 sts at the beg of the next 2 rows. Cont to foll chart without further shaping until row 131/135 has been worked.
Next row (WS) **shape neck:** p47/55, leave rem sts on a spare needle, turn, and, working on this first set of sts only, cast off 4 sts at the beg of the next row, 3 sts at the beg of the next alt row, and 2 sts at the beg of the foll 2 alt rows. Work 7 rows straight, dec 1 st at neck edge on next row, work 6 rows. Next row

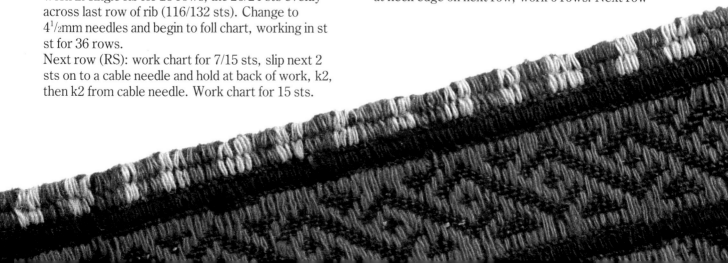

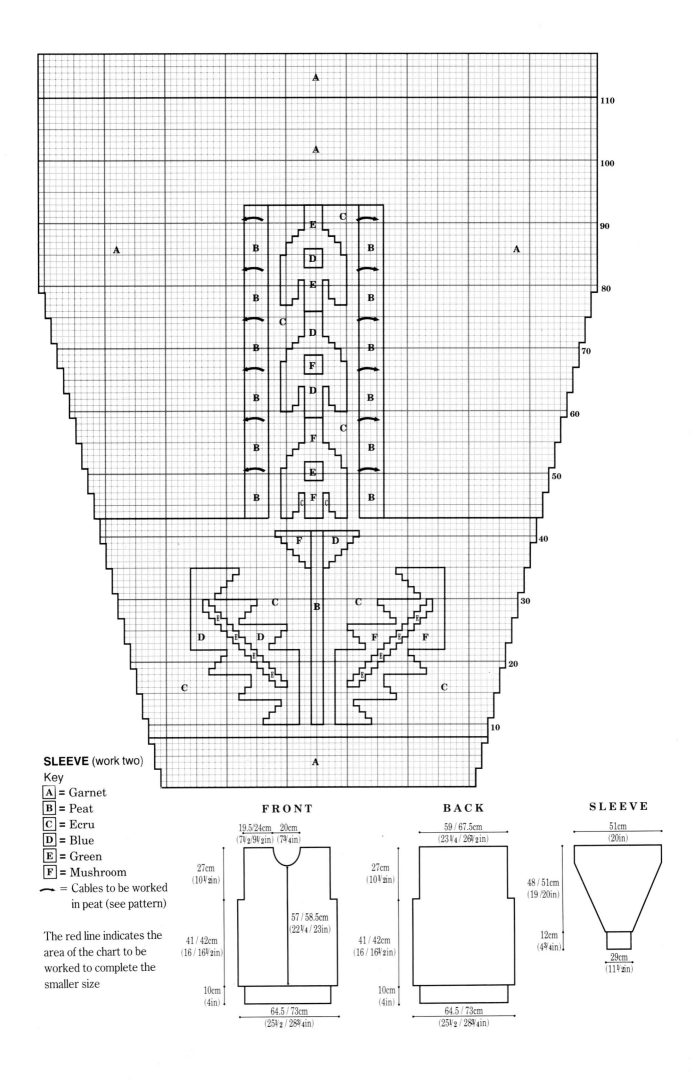

110

100

90

80

70

60

50

40

30

20

10

SLEEVE (work two)

Key

A = Garnet

B = Peat

C = Ecru

D = Blue

E = Green

F = Mushroom

⌒ = Cables to be worked
in peat (see pattern)

The red line indicates the
area of the chart to be
worked to complete the
smaller size

FRONT

19.5/24cm 20cm
(7½/9½in) (7¾in)

27cm
(10½in)

57 / 58.5cm
(22¼ / 23in)

41 / 42cm
(16 / 16½in)

10cm
(4in)

64.5 / 73cm
(25½ / 28¾in)

BACK

59 / 67.5cm
(23¼ / 26½in)

27cm
(10½in)

41 / 42cm
(16 / 16½in)

10cm
(4in)

64.5 / 73cm
(25½ / 28¾in)

SLEEVE

51cm
(20in)

48 / 51cm
(19 /20in)

12cm
(4¾in)

29cm
(11½in)

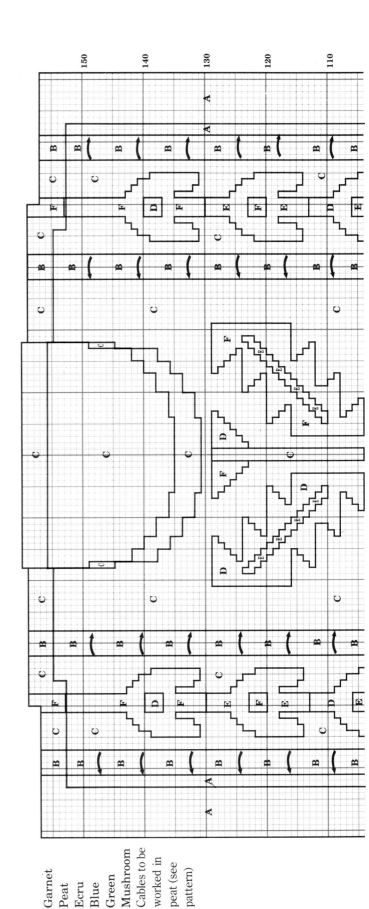

(WS) shape shoulders: cast off 17/21 sts at the beg of
the next row, work 1 row, cast off rem 18/22 sts.
Return to held sts and slip centre 12 sts on to a spare
needle. Work neck and shoulder shapings to match
other side of neck.

BACK

Work as for front, ignoring neck shaping, until row
153/157 is complete. **Shape shoulders:** cast off
17/21 sts at the beg of the next 2 rows, and 18/22 sts
at the beg of the foll 2 rows. Cast off rem 36 sts.

SLEEVES

Using 3³/₄mm needles and peat, cast on 48 sts. Work
in single rib for 30 rows, inc 4 sts evenly across last
row of rib (52 sts). Change to 4¹/₂mm needles and
begin to foll chart, inc 1 st each end of every fourth
row until you have 92 sts. **At the same time**, when
you have 76 sts and chart indicates cable row, place
cables as follows. Next row (RS): work chart for 27
sts. Slip next 2 sts on to a cable needle and hold at
back, k2, then k2 from cable needle. Work chart for
15 sts. Slip next 2 sts on to a cable needle and hold at
front of work, k2, then k2 from cable needle. This
sets your cable directions. Work cables as set on the
foll 4 eighth rows as indicated by arrows on chart.
When increases are complete, work straight for
30/37 rows. Cast off loosely. Join shoulder seams.

NECKBAND

Using a 3¹/₄mm circular needle and peat, pick up and
knit 114 sts evenly around the neck. Work in single
rib for 4 rows, ending at centre front. **Make collar
opening**: turn, rib back to centre front, turn, rib
back to centre front. Cont working in this way for a
further 24 rows. Cast off in rib.

MAKING UP

Join side and sleeve seams using a flat seam.

Key
A = Garnet
B = Peat
C = Ecru
D = Blue
E = Green
F = Mushroom
(= Cables to be
worked in
peat (see
pattern)

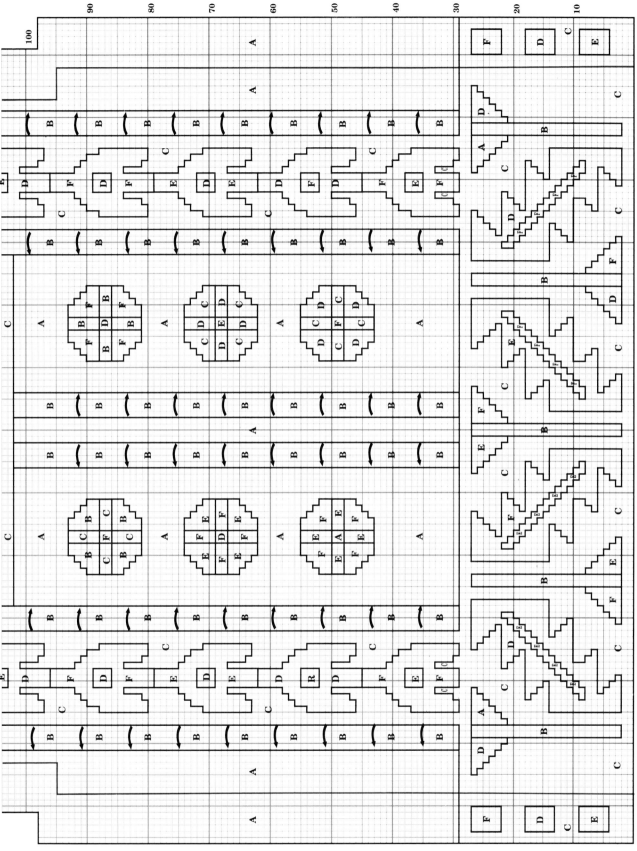

BACK AND FRONT

The red line indicates the area of the chart to be worked for the smaller size

MINNEHAHA CARDIGAN

THIS 4-PLY CARDIGAN is decorated with beadwork that is reminiscent of the motifs found on North American Indian dress. The lace and cable patterning is very simple to work, and the pattern knits up for both summer and winter in 4-ply mercerized cotton or wool. The sizes quoted are to fit bust sizes 86/92cm (32/34in).

Materials

Melinda Coss 4-ply wool – 350gm khaki **or** 4-ply mercerized cotton – 450gm ivory. Small plastic beads in assorted colours; 15 polished shells for buttons.

Needles

One pair of 2mm needles; one pair of 2³/₄mm needles; one cable needle.

Tension

Using 2³/₄mm needles and measured over st st, 32 sts and 40 rows = 10cm square.

BACK

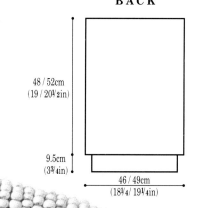

48 / 52cm
(19 / 20½in)

9.5cm
(3³/₄in)

46 / 49cm
(18¼/ 19¼in)

BACK

Using 2mm needles, cast on 142/152 sts. Work in single twisted rib (k in back of k sts) for 38 rows, inc 6 sts evenly across last row of rib (148/158 sts). Change to 2³/₄mm needles and begin to work pattern as follows.

Row 1 (RS): p5/10, *(p2, k2, yo, k2tog, p2) twice *, p6, k4, p6, rep from * to *, p6, k4, p9, k4, p9, k4, p6, rep from * to *, p6, k4, p6, rep from * to *, p5/10.

Row 2: k5/10, **(k2, p2, yo, p2tog, k2) twice**, k6, p4, k6, rep from ** to **, k6, p4, k9, p4, k9, p4, k6, rep from ** to **, k6, p4, k6, rep from ** to **, k5/10.

Rows 3 and 5: as row 1.

Rows 4 and 6: as row 2.

Row 7: p5/10, (p2, slip the next 2 sts on to a cable needle and hold at front of work, k2, then k2 from cable needle (c4f) p2) twice, p6, slip the next 2 sts on to a cable needle and hold at back of work, k2, then k2 from cable needle (c4b), p6, (p2, c4f, p2) twice, p6, c4b, p9, c4b, p9, c4b, p6, (p2, c4f, p2) twice, p6, c4b, p6, (p2, c4f, p2) twice, p5/10.

Row 8: as row 2.

Rows 9, 11 and 13: as row 1.

Rows 10, 12, 14 and 16: as row 2.

Row 15: p5/10, *(p2, k2, yo, k2tog, p2) twice*, p6, c4b, p6, rep from * to *, p6, c4b, p9, c4b, p9, c4b, p6, rep from * to *, p6, c4b, p6, rep from * to *, p5/10.

These 16 rows make up the pattern. Rep them 8/9 times more.

Next row (RS): starting with a k row, work 8 rows in st st. **Begin yoke.**

Row 1 (RS): p11/16, k4, *(p12, k4) 3 times*, (p9, k4) twice, rep from * to *, p11/16.

Row 2: k11/16, p4, **(k12, p4) 3 times**, (k9, p4) twice, rep from ** to **, k11/16. Rep these 2 rows twice more.

Row 7: p11/16; c4b, (p12, c4b) 3 times, (p9, c4b) twice, (p12, c4b) 3 times, p11/16.

Row 8: as row 2.

Cont rep these 8 rows until work measures 57.5/ 61.5cm. Cast off all sts.

RIGHT FRONT

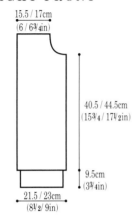

15.5 / 17cm
(6 / 6³/₄in)

40.5 / 44.5cm
(15³/₄ / 17¹/₂in)

9.5cm
(3³/₄in)

21.5 / 23cm
(8¹/₂ / 9in)

RIGHT FRONT

With 2mm needles, cast on 66/71 sts and work in single twisted rib for 38 rows, inc 3 sts evenly across last row of rib (69/74 sts). Change to 2³/₄mm needles and begin to work pattern as follows.

Row 1 (RS): p6, k4, p6, *(p2, k2, yo, k2tog, p2) twice*, p6, k4, p6, rep from * to *, p5/10.

Row 2: k5/10, **(k2, p2, yo, p2tog, k2) twice**, k6, p4, k6, rep from ** to **, k6, p4, k6.

Rows 3 and 5: as row 1.

Row 4 and 6: as row 2.

Row 7: p6, c4b, p6, (p2, c4f, p2) twice, p6, c4b, p6, (p2, c4f, p2) twice, p5/10.

Row 8: as row 2.

Rows 9, 11 and 13: as row 1.

Rows 10, 12 and 14: as row 2.

Row 15: p6, c4b, p6, (p2, k2, yo, k2tog, p2) twice, p6, c4b, p6, (p2, k2, yo, k2tog, p2) twice, p5/10.

Row 16: as row 2.

Rep the last 16 rows 8/9 times more. Next row (RS): starting with a k row, work 8 rows in st st. **Begin yoke.**

Row 1 (RS): p6, (k4, p12) 3 times, k4, p11/16.

Row 2: k11/16, (p4, k12) 3 times, p4, k6. Rep these 2 rows twice more.

Row 7: p6, (c4b, p12) 3 times, c4b, k11/16.

Row 8: as row 2.

Cont rep these 8 rows until work measures 50/ 54cm, ending with a WS row. **Shape neck** (RS): keeping in patt, cast off 5 sts at the beg of the next row and dec 1 st at the same edge on the next 14 rows. Work straight in patt until front matches back to shoulder. Cast off remaining 50/55 sts.

LEFT FRONT

Work rib as for right front. Change to 2³/₄mm needles and work pattern as follows.

Row 1 (RS): p5/10, *(p2, k2, yo, k2tog, p2) twice*, p6, k4, p6, rep from * to *, p6, k4, p6.

Row 2: k6, p4, k6, **(k2, p2, yo, p2tog, k2) twice**, k6, p4, k6, rep from ** to **, k5/10.

Rows 3 and 5: as row 1.

Rows 4 and 6: as row 2.

Row 7: p5/10, (p2, c4f, p2) twice, p6, c4b, p6, (p2, c4f, p2) twice, p6, c4b, p9.

Row 8: as row 2.

Rows 9, 11 and 13: as row 1.

Rows 10, 12 and 14: as row 2.

Row 15: p5/10, (p2, k2, yo, k2tog, p2) twice, p6, c4b, p6, (p2, k2, yo, k2tog, p2) twice, p6, c4b, p6.

Row 16: as row 2.

Repeat the last 16 rows 8/9 times more.

Next row (RS): starting with a k row, work 8 rows in st st. **Begin yoke.**

Row 1 (RS): p11/16, (k4, p12) 3 times, k4, p6.

Row 2: k6, p4, (k12, p4) 3 times, k11/16. Rep these 2 rows twice more.

Row 7: k11/16, (c4b, k12) 3 times, c4b, k6.

Row 8: as row 2.

Cont rep these 8 rows until work measures 50/ 54cm, ending with a RS row. **Shape neck** (WS): keeping in patt, cast off 5 sts at the beg of the next row, then dec 1 st at the same edge on the next 14 rows. Work straight in patt until front matches back to shoulder. Cast off remaining 50/55 sts.

SLEEVE

30 /33cm
(11¾/ 13in)

36cm
(14in)

11cm
(4½in)

27.5 /30.5cm
(10¾/ 12in)

SLEEVES

(Both alike) With 2mm needles, cast on 77/84 sts.
Work in single twisted rib for 44 rows, inc 11/14 sts
evenly across the last row (88/98 sts). Change to
2¾/4mm needles and work pattern as follows.
Row 1 (RS): p10/15, k4, p6, *(p2, k2, yo, k2tog, p2)
twice*, p6, k4, p6, rep from * to *, p6, k4, p10/15.
Row 2: k10/15, p4, k6, **(k2, p2, yo, p2tog, k2)
twice**, k6, p4, k6, rep from ** to **, k6, p4,
k10/15.
Rows 3 and 5: as row 1.
Rows 4 and 6: as row 2.
Row 7: p10/15, c4b, p6, (p2, c4f, p2) twice, p6, c4b,
p6, (p2, c4f, p2) twice, p6, c4b, p10/15.
Row 8: as row 2.
Rows 9, 11 and 13: as row 1.
Rows 10, 12 and 14: as row 2.
Row 15: p10/15, c4b, p6, *(p2, c4f, p2) twice*, p6,
c4b, p6, rep from * to *, p6, c4b, p10/15.
Row 16: as row 2.
Rep the last 16 rows 9 times more. **At the same
time** inc 1 st each end of every 23rd row, 4 times
(96/106 sts). Cont without further shaping until
patterning is complete. Cast off all sts.

BUTTONBAND

With 2mm needles, cast on 10 sts. Work in k1, p1 rib
until band fits neatly to neck edge when slightly
stretched.

LACE BUTTONHOLE BAND

With 2mm needles, cast on 8 sts.
Row 1: sl1, k2, yo, p2tog, (yo) twice, p2tog, k1tbl.
Row 2: sl1, k2, p1, k2, yo, p2tog, k1tbl.
Row 3: sl1, k2, yo, p2tog, k1, (yo) twice, p2tog,
k1tbl.
Row 4: sl1, k2, p1, k3, yo, p2tog, k1tbl.
Row 5: sl1, k2, yo, p2tog, k2, (yo) twice, p2tog,
k1tbl.
Row 6: sl1, k2, p1, k4, yo, p2tog, k1tbl.
Row 7: sl1, k2, yo, p2tog, k5, k1tbl.
Row 8: cast off 3 sts, k4, yo, p2tog, k1tbl.
Rep the last 8 rows until border is 2 rows shorter
than buttonband, k 2 rows. Cast off.
Join shoulder seams, join buttonband to left front and
lace border to right front.

COLLAR

With 2mm needles and WS facing, pick up and knit 10
sts across top of button band, 34 sts up left front, 48
sts across back neck, 34 sts down right front and 8
sts across lace band (134 sts). Work pattern as
follows.
Row 1 (RS): knit.
Row 2: k6, p122, k6.
Rep these last 2 rows until work measures 8cm.
Work 6 rows in garter st. Cast off.

BORDER

Cast on 8 sts and work as for buttonhole band for 264
rows. Cast off. Stitch carefully into position.

BEADING

Cut a length of knitting wool and, using a needle with
a very slim head, knot the end of the yarn and bring it
through to the front of your work at the point where
the cable crosses. Thread 6 small beads of one
colour only on to your needle and lay these across
the cable. Take the needle down at the other side of
the cable and bring it back up just above the first
strand of beads. Rep the process 3 times, using
colours of your choice. Work in this way over
random cable knots. Using the same method, sew
squares of coloured beads across the yoke band in
between the cables (see the photograph). Then,
working from the centre, sew a circle of beads on
each side of the collar.
Join sleeve and side seams, sew shells for buttons
opposite every alternate hole on lace border.

NIGERIAN SWEATER

THE BOLD DESIGNS and bright colours of African textiles provide an endless resource for modern textile design. This particular pattern was taken from Nigeria, where it appeared on an embroidery commissioned by the Church Missionary Society. The sweater, which will fit up to 92cm (36in) bust, is worked in alpaca.

Materials

Melinda Coss alpaca – 500gm bright blue (A); 50gm scarlet (B); 50gm white (C); 50gm yellow; 50gm lime green; 50gm black; 50gm mauve.

Needles

One pair of 3¹/₄mm needles; one pair of 4mm needles. Stitch holders.

Tension

Using 4mm needles and measured over st st, 22 sts and 23 rows = 10cm square.

FRONT

With 3¹/₄mm needles and A, cast on 111 sts. Work in k1, p1 rib for 8cm. Change to 4mm needles and work 36 rows in st st, **at the same time** inc 1 st at each end of next and every foll eighth row until you have 121 sts.

Next row: begin to foll chart, working in st st throughout. Work 90 rows of chart *. **Shape neck.** Row 91 of chart: work patt for 44 sts, turn. Cont working from chart, **at the same time** dec 1 st at neck edge on every row until you have 35 sts. Work 8 rows without shaping. Cast off. Slip centre 33 sts on to a st holder, rejoin yarn to rem sts and work patt to end. Work second side of neck to match first.

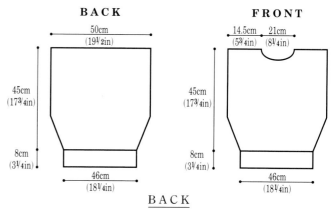

BACK

Work as for front to *. Cont to foll chart to top, omitting neck shaping. When chart is complete, cast off all sts.

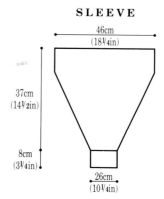

SLEEVES

With 3¹/₄mm needles and A, cast on 53 sts. Work in k1, p1 rib for 8cm, inc 10 sts evenly across last row of rib (63 sts). Change to 4mm needles and work in st st, **at the same time** inc 1 st at each end of the third and every foll fourth row until you have 111 sts. Cont straight until sleeve measures 32cm, ending with a WS row.

Left sleeve: k40A, (k1B, k9A) twice, k1B, k to end in A. The motif is now placed. Foll the chart for the motif outlined in red for the top right side of the front, beg on row 67. Knit the 36 rows of the motif, then k 6 rows straight in A. Cast off loosely.

Right sleeve: the motif for this sleeve is the same as the motif on the top left side of neck, outlined in black on the chart. The outer edge of the original motif is worked in blue, but for the sleeve, read this as white, C. K 1 row in A, place motif (WS): p55A, p1C, p to end in A. K until motif is complete, k 10 rows straight in A. Cast off loosely. Join right shoulder seam.

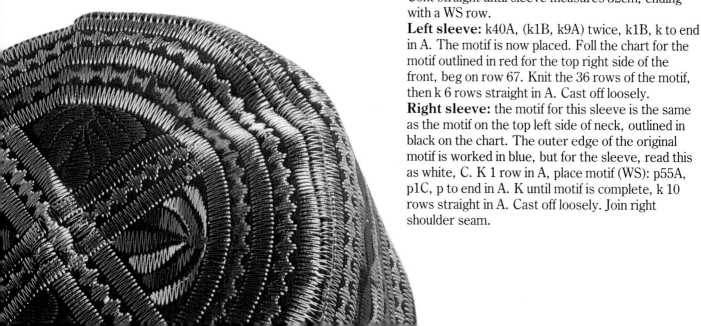

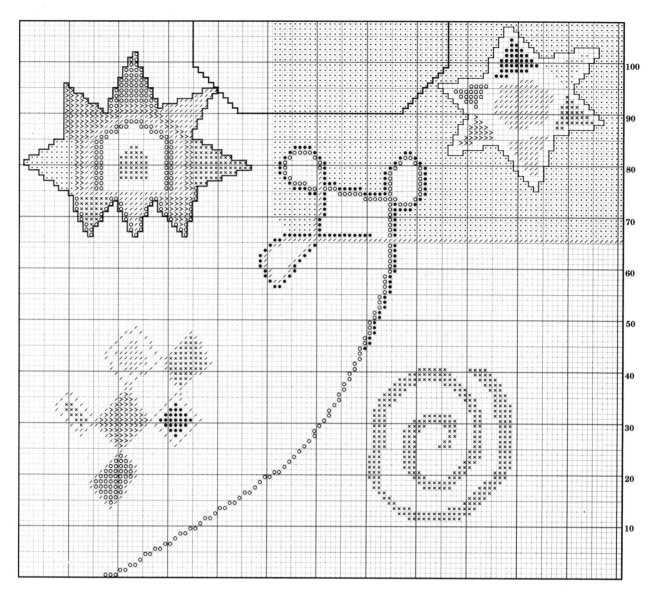

BACK AND FRONT

The motif outlined in red should be incorporated into the
left sleeve and the motif outlined in black should be
incorporated into the right sleeve (see pattern)

Key
☐ = blue (A)
Ⓞ = scarlet (B)
☒ = white (C)

⟋ = yellow
⟩ = lime green
· = mauve
● = black

NECKBAND

With 3¹/₄mm needles and B, pick up and k 24 sts
down left neck, 33 sts across front, 24 sts up right
neck, and 51 sts across back neck (132 sts). Work in
k1, pl rib for 7cm. Cast off using 4mm needles.

MAKING UP

Join left shoulder seam. Fold neckband inwards and
slip st cast-off edge to pick-up edge. Stitch sleeves
to jumper using narrow back stitch, and join sleeve
and side seams.

NOOTKA SILK JACKET

Materials

Melinda Coss tussah silk – 500gm cream; 125gm grey. 9 buttons, 1.5cm in diameter.

Needles

One pair of 3^1/$_4$mm needles; one pair of 4mm needles.

Tension

Using 4mm needles and measured over st st, 22 sts and 30 rows =10cm square.

BACK

Using 3^1/$_4$mm needles and cream, cast on 110 sts and work in k2, p2 rib for 10cm, inc 40 sts evenly across last row of rib (150 sts). Change to 4mm needles and, starting with a k row, begin working from back chart until it is complete. Cast off all sts.

BACK

66.5cm
(26^1/$_4$in)

10cm
(4in)

68cm
(26^3/$_4$in)

THIS DESIGN ORIGINATED with the North American Indian Nootka tribe, which lives mostly on Vancouver Island. The design is taken from a chieftain's hat made of cedar bark and spruce root. The embroidery, depicting a mythical thunderbird catching a whale, was originally worked with grass, but tussah silk seemed a more appropriate material for this stunning long-line jacket, which will fit 96–102cm (38–40in) chest.

RIGHT FRONT

Using 3¹/₄mm needles and cream, cast on 50 sts and
work 10cm in k2, p2 rib, inc 21 sts evenly across the
last row of rib (71 sts). Change to 4mm needles and,
starting with a k row, begin working from right front
chart, in st st, placing cables where indicated, to
neck shaping.

Next row (RS): cast off 6 sts at the beg of this row,
then dec 1 st at neck on the next 10 rows and the foll
5 alt rows (50 sts). Work a further 15 rows without
shaping and cast off all sts.

LEFT FRONT

Work as for right front, foll chart for right front but
reversing the image – i.e., work k rows from left to
right and p rows from right to left.

RIGHT/FRONT

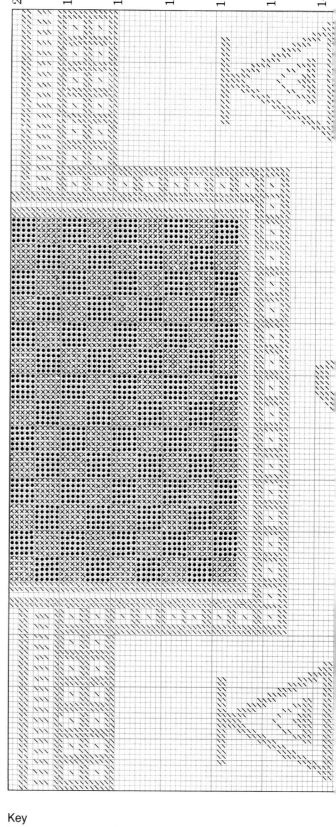

Key

☐ = cream

◪ = grey

⊡ = k on WS and p on RS in cream

☒ = k on RS and p on WS in cream

⟵ = c8F

130 120 110 100 90 80 70 60 50 40 30 20 10

GREY

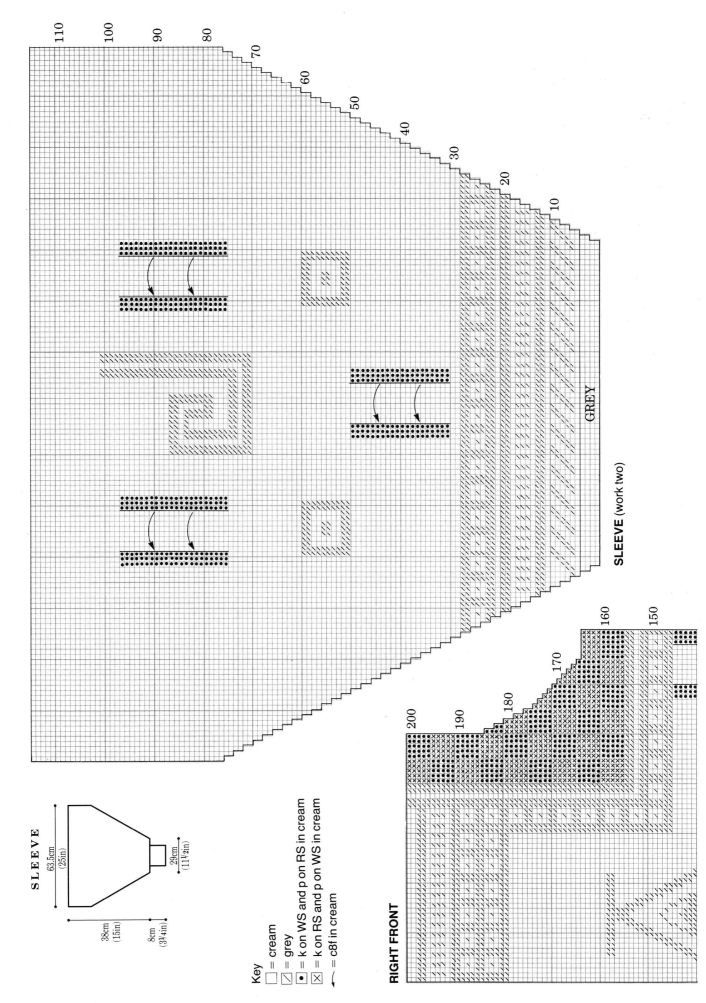

SLEEVE (work two)

GREY

110 100 90 80 70 60 50 40 30 20 10

SLEEVE

63.5cm (25in)

38cm (15in)

8cm (3¼in)

29cm (11½in)

Key

☐ = cream

◺ = grey

• = k on WS and p on RS in cream

☒ = k on RS and p on WS in cream

⌒ = c8f in cream

RIGHT FRONT

200 190 180 170 160 150

chart for sleeve, **at the same time** inc 1 st at each end of the third and every foll alt row until there are 140 sts. Work without further shaping until chart is complete. Cast off all sts. Join shoulder seams.

NECKBAND

Using 3^1/$_4$mm needles and cream and with RS facing, pick up and k 36 sts up right front neck, 50 sts across back neck and 36 sts down left front neck (122 sts). Work in k2, p2 rib for 9cm. Cast off loosely. Fold neckband inwards and slip st cast-off edge to pick-up edge.

BUTTONBAND

Using 3^1/$_4$mm needles and cream, cast on 10 sts and work in k2, p2 rib, until band fits neatly up left front from cast-on edge to top of neckband. Cast off sts loosely. Mark positions for 9 buttons, the first button 4 rows down from the top of the band, the last button 4 rows up from the bottom, spacing the others evenly between them.

BUTTONHOLE BAND

Work as for buttonband making buttonholes to correspond with markers as follows:
Row 1: k2, p2, cast off 2, k2, p2.
Row 2: k2, p2, cast on 2, k2, p2.

SLEEVES

(Both alike) Using 3^1/$_4$mm needles and cream, cast on 45 sts and work in k2, p2 rib for 8cm, inc 19 sts evenly across the last row of rib (64 sts). Change to 4mm needles and, starting with a k row, begin to foll

MAKING UP

Sew the front bands neatly into position. Join the sleeves to the body using a narrow back stitch, and use flat seams to join the sleeve and side seams. Sew on the buttons.

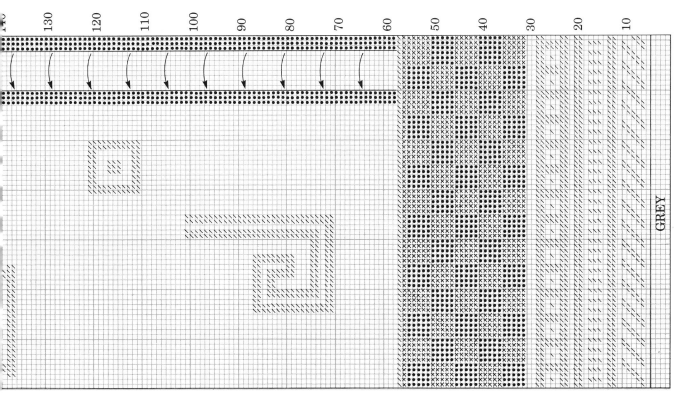

PERUVIAN ARAN
AND CHENILLE CARDIGAN

THIS DESIGN IS BASED on a Peruvian silk robe. The original silk was hand-spun and coloured with natural dyes, giving a rich and subtle colour contrast. The motifs represent animals and demons. The jacket will fit 96–112cm (38–44in) chest size.

Materials

Melinda Coss Aran wool – 650gm peat; Melinda Coss chenille (use double throughout) – 150gm cream; 75gm black; 50gm red; 50gm orange; 50gm purple. 9 buttons, 1.5cm in diameter.

Needles

One pair of 4^1/$_2$mm needles; one pair of 3^3/$_4$mm needles.

Tension

Using 4^1/$_2$mm needles and measured over st st, 18 sts and 23 rows = 10cm square.

BACK

Using 3^3/$_4$mm needles and peat, cast on 102 sts and work in fancy rib as follows:
Row 1: *k1, p1, k into front and back of next st, p1, rep from * to last st, k1.
Row 2: p1, *k1, p2tog, k1, p1, rep from * to end.
Repeat these 2 rows until work measures 10cm, inc 23 sts evenly across last row of rib (125 sts). Change to 4^1/$_2$mm needles and begin to foll chart for back in st st until it is complete. Cast off loosely.

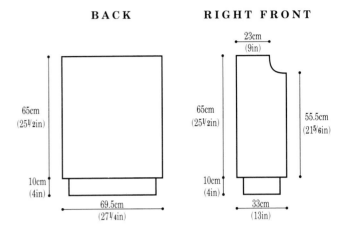

BACK   **RIGHT FRONT**

65cm (25^1/$_2$in)   23cm (9in)

65cm (25^1/$_2$in)   55.5cm (21^5/$_6$in)

10cm (4in)   10cm (4in)

69.5cm (27^1/$_4$in)   33cm (13in)

RIGHT FRONT

Using 3^3/$_4$mm needles and peat, cast on 52 sts and work in fancy rib as for back for 10cm, inc 8 sts evenly across last row of rib (60 sts). Change to 4^1/$_2$mm needles and begin to foll chart for right front to **neck shaping**.
Next row (RS): cast off 3 sts at the beg of this row, then dec 1 st at neck edge on the next 13 rows and the foll 2 alt rows, work 5 rows. Cast off.

LEFT FRONT

Work as for right front, reversing all shapings and following chart for left front.

SLEEVES

(Both alike) Using 3³/₄mm needles and peat, cast on 52 sts and work in fancy rib as for back for 8cm, inc 8 sts evenly across last row of rib (60 sts). Change to 4¹/₂mm needles and begin to foll chart for sleeve in st st. **At the same time** inc 1 st at each end of the fourth row and every foll fifth row until there are 96 sts. Cont until sleeve chart is complete. Cast off loosely. Join both shoulder seams.

NECKBAND

With RS facing and using 3³/₄mm needles and peat, pick up and k 88 sts evenly around neck edge. Work in fancy rib as for back for 9 rows. Cast off loosely in rib.

BUTTONBAND

Using 3³/₄mm needles and peat, cast on 8 sts and work in fancy rib until band fits neatly up left front from cast-on edge to top of neckband. Cast off. Sew neatly to left front and mark positions for 9 buttons, placing the first button 4 rows down from the top of the band and the last button 4 rows up from the bottom of the band, with the rest spaced evenly between them.

BUTTONHOLE BAND

Work as for buttonband, making buttonholes to correspond with buttons as follows:
Row 1: rib 3, cast off 2, rib 3.
Row 2: rib 3, cast on 2, rib 3.

MAKING UP

Set in sleeves, and join side and sleeve seams. Sew on buttons.

SLEEVE

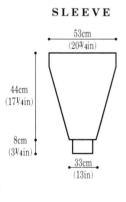

53cm
(20³/₄in)

44cm
(17¹/₄in)

8cm
(3¹/₄in)

33cm
(13in)

BACK, LEFT AND RIGHT FRONTS AND SLEEVES

The red lines indicate the area of the chart to be worked to complete the sleeves, and the front neck shaping and the areas of the chart to be worked to complete the right and left fronts

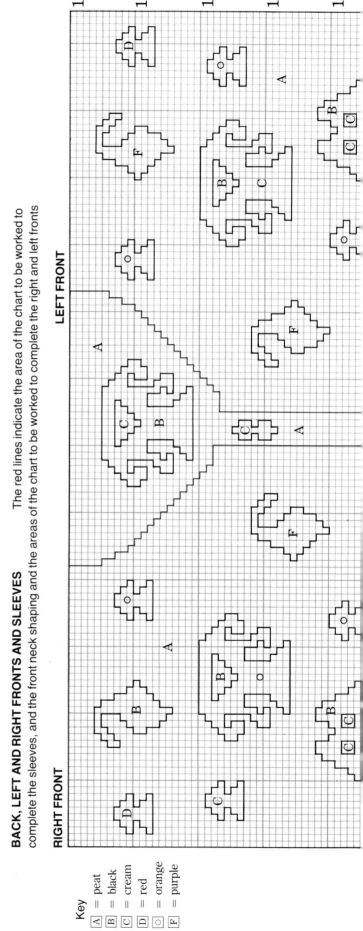

LEFT FRONT

RIGHT FRONT

Key
A = peat
B = black
C = cream
D = red
○ = orange
F = purple

PUEBLO JACKET

THIS STRIKING CHUNKY jacket was inspired by ancient Pueblo pottery originating in Arizona. Worked in stocking stitch using the intarsia method, the bold abstract images make this a perfect jacket for him or her, and it will fit up to chest size 112cm (44in).

Materials

Melinda Coss chunky – 800gm black; 500gm brick; 250gm white; 200gm turquoise; Melinda Coss Aran wool – 50gm black (for pocket lining). 5 wooden toggles, 5cm long.

Needles

One pair of 6¹/₂mm needles; one pair of 5¹/₂mm needles; one pair of 5mm needles. Medium sized crochet hook. Stitch holders.

Tension

Using 6¹/₂mm needles and measured over st st, 14 sts and 19 rows = 10cm square.

BACK

Using 5¹/₂mm needles and black, cast on 92 sts. Work in k2, p2 rib for 5cm, ending with a WS row. Change to 6¹/₂mm needles and begin to foll chart in st st. Work until chart is complete and leave sts on a spare needle, placing a marker 32 sts in at each side.

RIGHT FRONT

Using 5¹/₂mm needles and black, cast on 52 sts.
Row 1: k6, *p2, k2, rep from * to last 2 sts, p2.
Row 2: k2, *p2, k2, rep from * to last 6 sts, k6.
Rep these 2 rows until work measures 5cm. This sets the position for the garter st front band, which is not shown on the chart. Change to 6¹/₂mm needles and begin to foll chart in st st, adding 6 sts garter st border as already set on rib. Work straight to **neck shaping**.

Next row (RS): cast off 9 sts, k to end. Continue following the chart, dec 1 st at neck edge on every row 11 times (32 sts). Work straight until chart is complete and leave sts on a spare needle.

LEFT FRONT

With 5¹/₂mm needles and black, cast on 52 sts.
Row 1: *p2, k2, rep from * to last 8 sts, p2, k6.
Row 2: k6, *k2, p2, rep from * to last 2 sts, k2.
Rep these 2 rows until work measures 5cm. Change to 6¹/₂mm needles and begin to foll chart for left front, continuing k border as described in right front and working the chart in st st to neck shaping.

Next row (WS): cast off 9 sts, p to end. Shape neck as for right front.

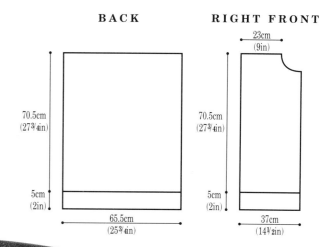

BACK

70.5cm
(27³/₄in)

5cm
(2in)

65.5cm
(25³/₄in)

RIGHT FRONT

23cm
(9in)

70.5cm
(27³/₄in)

5cm
(2in)

37cm
(14¹/₂in)

BACK

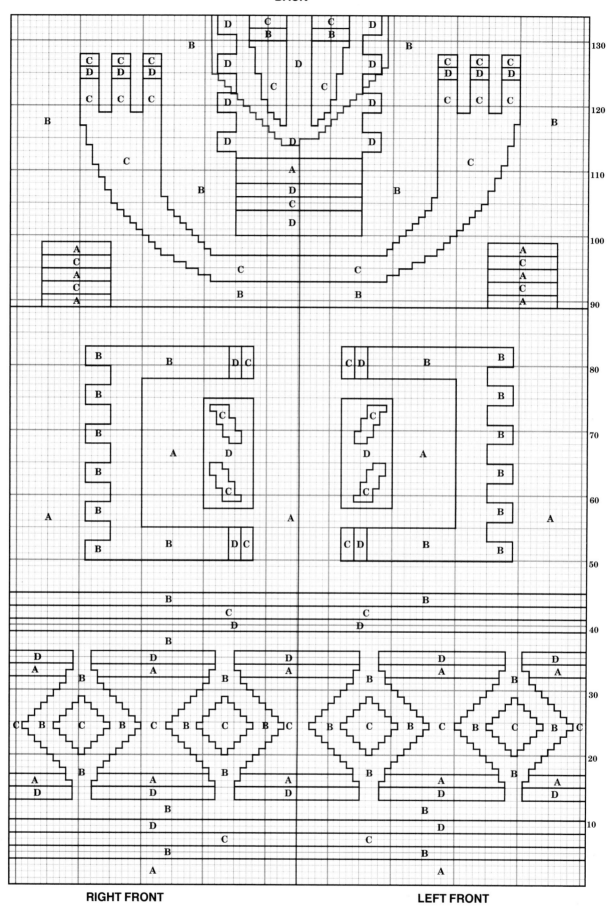

RIGHT FRONT   **LEFT FRONT**

The red line indicates the areas of the chart to be worked
to complete the left and right fronts

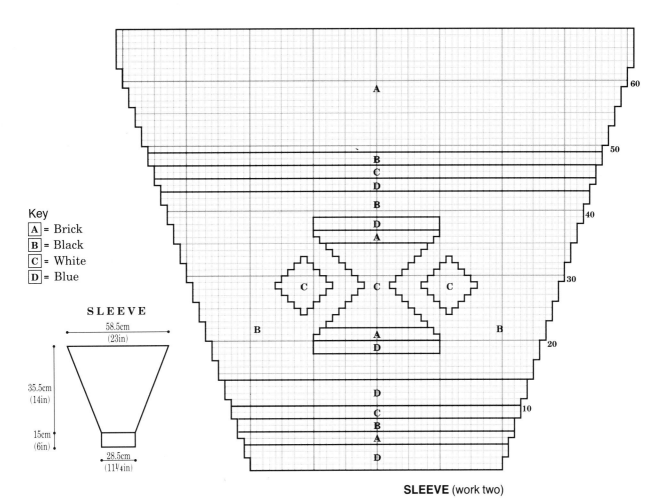

Key

A = Brick
B = Black
C = White
D = Blue

SLEEVE

58.5cm
(23in)

35.5cm
(14in)

15cm
(6in)

28.5cm
(11¼in)

60

50

40

30

20

10

A

B
C
D
B
D
A

C
C
C

B
B

A
D

D
C
B
A
D

SLEEVE (work two)

SLEEVES

Using 5¹/₂mm needles and black, cast on 40 sts and work in k2, p2 rib for 15cm. Change to 6¹/₂mm needles and begin to foll chart in st st, inc 1 st each end of every third row until you have 82 sts. Work straight until chart is complete. Cast off loosely.

COLLAR

Using 6¹/₂mm needles and black, cast on 10 sts. K every row, inc 1 st each end of every alt row (1 st in from the edge), until there are 18 sts. Now work one edge straight while increasing 1 st on every row on the other edge until there are 24 sts. Work straight for 72 rows. Now shape the other end to match, dec instead of inc until 10 sts rem. Cast off.

POCKET LINING

(Make 2) Using 5mm needles and working to a tension of 18 sts and 23 rows to 10cm square, cast on 30 sts in black Aran wool. Work in st st for 30cm. Cast off.

MAKING UP

Knit one shoulder seam together. Cast off the centre 28 sts on the back neck, then knit the second shoulder seam together. Join sleeves to jacket. Join sleeve seam, reversing stitching half way down the cuff to allow for fold back. Join side seams, leaving an opening 13cm deep each side at a comfortable position for a pocket. Join the remaining side seams.

Sew cast-on edge of pocket lining to front edge of pocket opening and cast-off edge to back edge of pocket opening. Sew up pocket side seams. Sew on collar by joining shaped edge to neck edge. Sew 5 toggles evenly up the centre of the buttonband (left band for women, right for men). With a crochet hook and black Aran wool, make 5 single chains, 8cm long. Attach these opposite the toggles, placing them where the front band joins the jacket front.

TURKISH DELIGHT

INSPIRED BY MOTIFS found on Turkish carpets, this Aran-weight cropped jacket with a shawl collar is worked in stocking stitch using the intarsia method. It will fit up to bust size 92–96cm (36–38in).

Materials

Melinda Coss Aran wool – 650gm royal blue; 75gm brown; 50gm gold; 50gm rust; 50gm green; 25gm fawn. 6 wooden toggles, 3cm long.

Needles

One pair of $5^1/_2$mm; one pair of $4^1/_2$mm needles.

Tension

Using $5^1/_2$mm needles and measured over st st, 19 sts and 24 rows = 10cm square.

BACK

With $4^1/_2$mm needles and royal blue, cast on 107 sts and work in k1, p1 rib for 2cm. Change to $5^1/_2$mm needles and begin to foll chart in st st until 66 rows have been worked. **Shape armholes:** cast off 5 sts at the beg of the next 2 rows. Work straight from chart until 104 rows have been completed. **Shape neck** (RS): k41 and leave rem sts on a spare needle. Working on this first set of sts only, dec 1 st at neck edge on the next 12 rows. Work 1 row. **Shape shoulders.**

Next row (RS): cast off 15 sts at the beg of this row. Work 1 row, cast off rem 14 sts. With RS facing, rejoin yarn to remaining sts. Cast off centre 15 sts, work to end. Dec 1 st at neck edge on next 12 rows. Shape shoulder: cast off 15 sts at the beg of the next row, work 1 row. Cast off rem 14 sts.

BACK

[Diagram showing back measurements:
15cm (6in), 20.5cm (8in) at top;
22.5cm (8¾in);
27.5cm (10¾in);
2cm (¾in);
56cm (22in)]

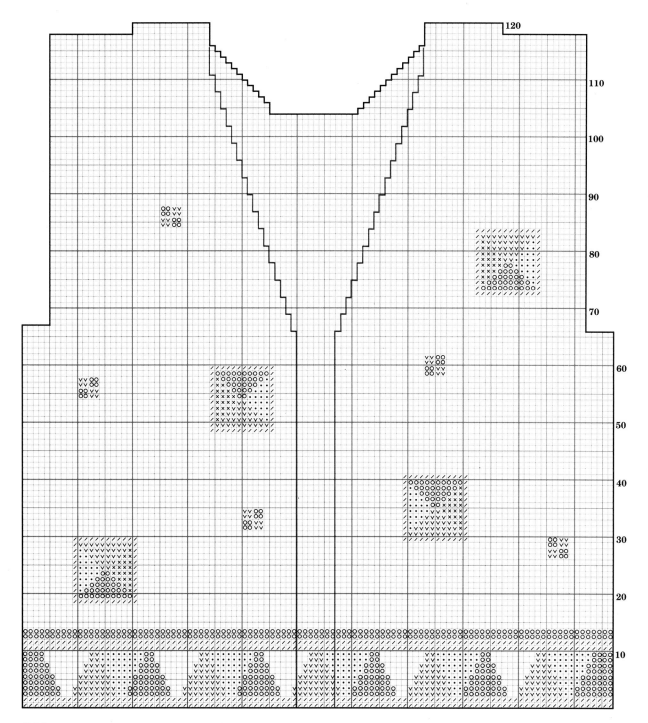

BACK AND LEFT AND RIGHT FRONTS

The red lines indicate the areas to be worked to complete the left and right fronts

LEFT FRONT

With 4¹/₂mm needles and royal blue, cast on 50 sts. Work in k1, p1 rib for 2cm. Change to 5¹/₂mm needles and begin to foll chart for left front, working in st st until 66 rows have been completed. Next row (RS): cast off 5 sts at the beg of this row, follow chart to last 3 sts, k2tog, k1. Cont to foll chart, dec 1 st (1 st in as set) at the neck edge on the 15 foll third rows (29 sts). Work straight to **shoulder shaping**. Row 119 (RS): cast off 15 sts at the beg of this row. Work 1 row. Cast off rem 14 sts.

RIGHT FRONT

Work as for left front but follow chart for right front and reverse all shapings.

LEFT FRONT

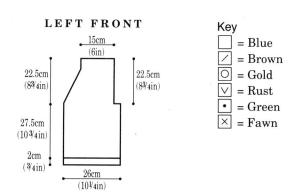

15cm
(6in)

22.5cm
(8³/4in)

22.5cm
(8³/4in)

27.5cm
(10³/4in)

2cm
(³/4in)

26cm
(10¹/4in)

Key

☐	= Blue
⟋	= Brown
◯	= Gold
⋁	= Rust
•	= Green
✕	= Fawn

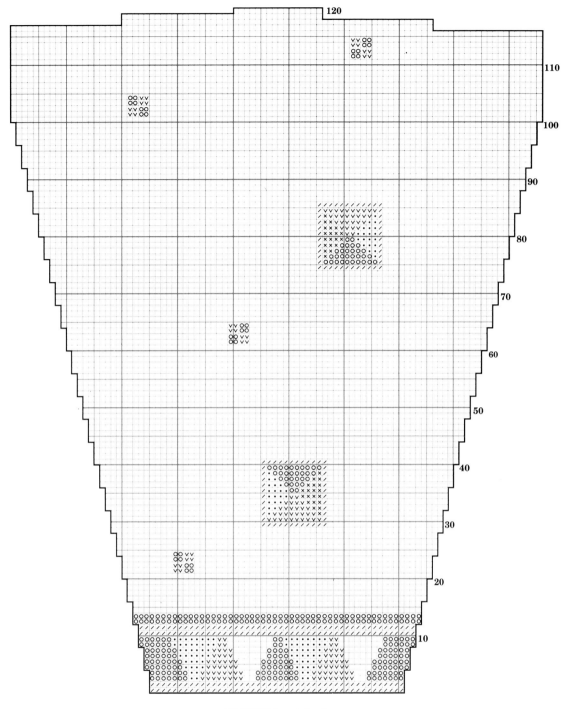

SLEEVE (work two)

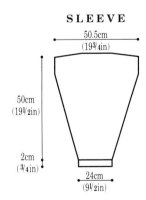

SLEEVE

50.5cm
(19¾in)

50cm
(19½in)

2cm
(¾in)

24cm
(9½in)

SLEEVES

(Both alike) With 4½mm needles and royal blue, cast on 46 sts and work in k1, p1 rib for 2cm. Change to 5½mm needles and begin to foll chart for sleeve in st st, inc 1 st each end of row 5 and every foll fourth row until you have 96 sts. Work straight until 116 rows of chart have been completed. **Shape sleeve top**. Row 117: cast off 20 sts at the beg of the next 4 rows. Cast off rem 16 sts.

COLLAR

Right section: with 5½mm needles and brown, cast on 3 sts and work from chart in st st, shaping as indicated. Mark the shoulder point with a coloured thread.

CENTRE BACK

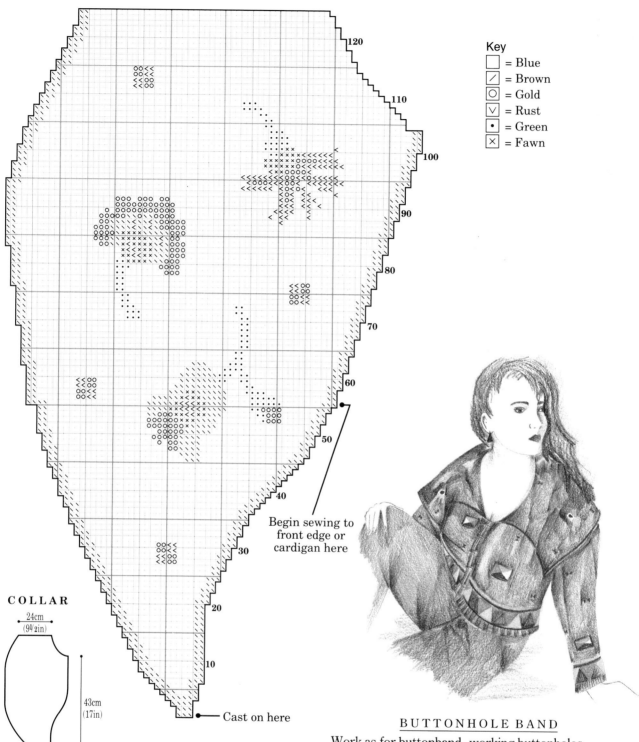

120

110

100

90

80

70

60

50

40

30

20

10

Begin sewing to
front edge or
cardigan here

Cast on here

COLLAR

24cm
(9½in)

43cm
(17in)

Left section: work as for right section but reverse
all shapings.

BUTTONBAND

With 4½mm needles and blue, cast on 7 sts and work
in single rib until band fits neatly, when slightly
stretched, to beg of neck shaping. Mark positions for
6 buttons, the first 4 rows from the bottom of the
band and the last 3 rows from the top of the
band. Space the other 4 buttons evenly between them.

BUTTONHOLE BAND

Work as for buttonband, working buttonholes
opposite marked positions: rib 3, k2tog, rib 2. On
return row, cast on 2 sts over those cast off on
previous row.

MAKING UP

Sew the front bands into place using a flat seam. Join
shoulder seams, and use a flat seam to attach the
sleeves. Join the side and sleeve seams. Join both
halves of collar using a flat seam, and pin this seam to
centre back of cardigan. Join collar neatly to
cardigan, sewing as far as the point marked on chart.
Sew on buttons.